Pathfinder®Guides

# North Wales, Snowdon and Offa's Dyke

## Walks

*Originally compiled by
Brian Conduit and Tom Hutton
Revised by Neil Coates
and Tom Hutton*

(1) start to END
(2) North to North
(3) RED to Red

Acknowledgements
My thanks to John Ellis Roberts and Gareth Davies, Head Wardens of the
Snowdonia National Park, for their useful advice, and to Denbighshire and
Flintshire County Councils for providing me with invaluable leaflets and
information. Particular thanks to my old friend Hugh Thomas, member of the
Ogwen Mountain Rescue Team, for accompanying me on two of the toughest
walks in the book. The publishers also thank Mr Derick Cuthbert of the Conwy
Valley Ramblers for helping to update information.

Text:                     Brian Conduit, Tom Hutton, Neil Coates
                          Revised text for 2009 edition, Tom Hutton
Photography:              Brian Conduit, Neil Coates
Editorial:                Ark Creative (UK) Ltd
Design:                   Ark Creative (UK) Ltd

ISBN:  978-1-85458-541-7

While every care has been taken to ensure the accuracy of the route directions,
the publishers cannot accept responsibility for errors or omissions, or for changes
in details given. The countryside is not static: hedges and fences can be removed,
field boundaries can alter, footpaths can be rerouted and changes in ownership
can result in the closure or diversion of some concessionary paths. Also, paths
that are easy and pleasant for walking in fine conditions may become slippery,
muddy and difficult in wet weather, while stepping stones across rivers and
streams may become impassable.
    If you find an inaccuracy in either the text or maps, please write to Crimson
Publishing at the address below.

First published 1998
Revised and reprinted 2001, 2004, 2006, 2007, 2009.

This edition first published in Great Britain 2009 by Crimson Publishing, a
division of:
**Crimson Business Ltd,**
Westminster House, Kew Road, Richmond, Surrey, TW9 2ND

Printed in Singapore. 6/09

**Front cover:** Clapper Bridge and Tyrau Mawr
**Previous page:** Chirk Castle

# Contents

| | | |
|---|---|---|
| Keymap | | 4 |
| At-a-glance... walks chart | | 6 |
| Introduction | | 8 |
| Walks | | |

**1** Greenfield Valley Heritage Park — 12

**2** Great Orme — 14

**3** Caergwrle and Hope — 16

**4** Rhyl and Rhuddlan — 18

**5** Denbigh and the Ystrad Valley — 20

**6** Hawarden Park — 23

**7** Pistyll Rhaeadr — 26

**8** Capel Curig — 28

**9** Tal-y-llyn Lake — 30

**10** Cregennen Lakes and Arthog Waterfalls — 32

**11** Ty Mawr and the Pontcysyllte Aqueduct — 34

**12** Chirk and the River Ceiriog — 37

**13** Prestatyn Hillside — 40

**14** Llyn y Gader and Beddgelert Forest — 43

**15** Elwy Valley — 46

**16** Llyn Padarn — 49

**17** Lledr Valley — 52

**18** Vale of Ffestiniog — 55

**19** Llanrwst, Gwydyr Forest and Trefriu — 58

**20** Rhaeadr Mawddach and Pistyll Cain — 61

**21** Penmaenmawr and the Druid's Circle — 64

**22** Penycloddiau and Moel Arthur — 67

**23** Llyn Brenig — 70

**24** Llangollen, Castell Dinas Bran and Valle Crucis Abbey — 73

**25** Cilcain and Moel Famau — 77

**26** Bwlch Maen Gwynedd — 80

**27** Carnedd Dafydd — 84

**28** Snowdon via the Watkin Path — 87

Further Information — 90

The National Trust; The Ramblers'
Association; Walkers and the Law;
Global Positioning System (GPS);
Glossary of Welsh Words; Countryside
Access Charter; Safety on the Hills;
Useful Organisations; Ordnance
Survey Maps

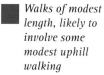

Short, easy walks

Walks of modest
length, likely to
involve some
modest uphill
walking

More challenging
walks which may
be longer and/or
over more rugged
terrain, often with
some stiff climbs

# Keymap

# Keymap

MOSTYN to
Dublin
Flynnongroyw
6 hrs

SCALE 1:357 143 or 1 INCH to about 5¾ MILES *1CM to 3.5KM*

0   2   4   6   8   10   KILOMETRES   15

0   2   4   6   MILES   8   10

KEYMAP HEIGHTS SHOWN IN METRES

*At-a-glance...*

| Walk | Page | Start | Nat. Grid Reference | Distance | Time | Highest Point |
|---|---|---|---|---|---|---|
| Bwlch Maen Gwynedd | 80 | Llandrillo | SJ 035371 | 7³/₄ miles (12.5km) | 5 hrs | 2,330ft (710m) |
| Caergwrle and Hope | 16 | Caergwrle | SJ 305574 | 4 miles (6.4km) | 2 hrs | 449ft (137m) |
| Capel Curig | 28 | Capel Curig National Park car park | SH 720582 | 4¹/₂ miles (7.2km) | 2¹/₂ hrs | 787ft (240m) |
| Carnedd Dafydd | 84 | Ogwen | SH 649603 | 7 miles (11.3km) | 6 hrs | 3,425ft (1,044m) |
| Chirk and the River Ceiriog | 37 | Chirk | SJ 291376 | 6 miles (9.7km) | 3 hrs | 823ft (251m) |
| Cilcain and Moel Famau | 77 | Loggerheads Country Park | SJ 198626 | 8 miles (12.9km) | 5 hrs | 1,818ft (554m) |
| Cregennen Lakes and Arthog Waterfalls | 32 | National Trust car park | SH 657143 | 4 miles (6.5km) | 2¹/₂ hrs | 837ft (255m) |
| Denbigh and the Ystrad Valley | 20 | Denbigh | SJ 050661 | 5 miles (8km) | 2¹/₂ hrs | 499ft (152m) |
| Elwy Valley | 46 | Llanfair Talhaiarn | SH 927702 | 5 miles (8km) | 2¹/₂ hrs | 942ft (287m) |
| Great Orme | 14 | Great Orme Country Park | SH 765833 | 3¹/₂ miles (5.6km) | 2 hrs | 679ft (207m) |
| Greenfield Valley Heritage Park | 12 | Greenfield Valley Heritage Park | SJ 197775 | 2¹/₂ miles (4km) | 1¹/₂ hrs | 239ft (73m) |
| Hawarden Park | 23 | Hawarden | SJ 316657 | 5¹/₂ miles (8.9km) | 2¹/₂ hrs | 311ft (95m) |
| Llangollen, Castell Dinas Bran & Valle Crucis Abbey | 73 | Llangollen | SJ 215421 | 8¹/₂ miles (13.7km) | 5 hrs | 1,050ft (320m) |
| Llanrwst, Gwydyr Forest and Trefriw | 58 | Llanrwst | SH 798616 | 6 miles (9.7km) | 3 hrs | 607ft (185m) |
| Lledr Valley | 52 | Dolwyddelan | SH 737521 | 6¹/₂ miles (10.5km) | 3 hrs | 689ft (210m) |
| Llyn Brenig | 70 | Llyn Brenig Visitor Centre | SH 967546 | 10 miles (16.1km) | 4¹/₂ hrs | 1,476ft (450m) |
| Llyn Padarn | 49 | Llanberis, village car park | SH 577604 | 5¹/₂ miles (8.9km) | 3 hrs | 725ft (221m) |
| Llyn y Gader and Beddgelert Forest | 43 | Rhyd-Ddu, National Park car park | SH 571525 | 5 miles (8km) | 2¹/₂ hrs | 1,053ft (321m) |
| Penmaenmawr and the Druid's Circle | 64 | Penmaenmawr town centre | SH 719762 | 4¹/₂ miles (7.2km) | 2¹/₂ hrs | 1,319ft (402m) |
| Penycloddiau and Moel Arthur | 67 | Llangwyfan car park | SJ 139667 | 7¹/₂ miles (12.1km) | 3¹/₂ hrs | 1,460ft (445m) |
| Pistyll Rhaeadr | 26 | Tan-y-pistyll | SJ 074294 | 3 miles (4.8km) | 1¹/₂ hrs | 1,378ft (420m) |
| Prestatyn Hillside | 40 | Prestatyn Hillside Viewpoint | SJ 074819 | 5¹/₂ miles (8.75km) | 3 hrs | 656ft (200m) |
| Rhaeadr Mawddach and Pistyll Cain | 61 | Ganllwyd, National Trust car park | SH 727243 | 7 miles (11.3km) | 3¹/₂ hrs | 623ft (190m) |
| Rhyl and Rhuddlan | 18 | Rhyl, Foryd Bridge | SH 996806 | 5¹/₂ miles (8.75km) | 2¹/₂ hrs | 23ft (7m) |
| Snowdon via the Watkin Path | 87 | Pont Bethania car park | SH 627506 | 9 miles (14.5km) | 7 hrs | 3,560ft (1,085m) |
| Tal-y-llyn Lake | 30 | Tal-y-llyn | SH 714094 | 3¹/₂ miles (5.6km) | 2 hrs | 791ft (241m) |
| Ty Mawr and the Pontcysyllte Aqueduct | 34 | Ty Mawr Country Park | SJ 283414 | 6 miles (9.7km) | 3 hrs | 492ft (150m) |
| Vale of Ffestiniog | 55 | Rhŷd-y-sarn parking and picnic area | SH 690422 | 5¹/₂ miles (8.9km) | 3 hrs | 597ft (182m) |

## Comments

The halfway point on this walk is a pass through the long ridge of the Berwyn Mountains, 2,330 feet (710m) high.

As well as Hope Mountain, there are distant views of the Dee Estuary on this undemanding walk in the valley of the River Alyn.

There is much pleasant woodland and riverside walking beside the Llugwy, plus an outstanding view of Snowdon from the shores of Llynnau Mymbyr.

A demanding but satisfying walk that climbs to 3,425 feet (1,044m) and traverses one of the great ridges of the Carneddau to the summit of Carnedd Dafydd. The all round views from here are superb.

A walk through the parkland of Chirk Castle is followed by a dramatic descent into the lovely Ceiriog valley. Near the end you pass under an adjacent viaduct and aqueduct.

After a pleasant walk along the side of the wooded Alyn Valley and a visit to the village of Cilcain, you climb to the highest point on the Clwydian Hills, a magnificent viewpoint.

From many points there are grand views across the Mawddach Estuary and the walk through the wooded ravine beside the Arthog Waterfalls is outstanding.

Pleasant walking in the valley of the Afon Ystrad is followed by outstanding views of Denbigh Castle and across the Vale of Clwyd.

There are fine views over the Elwy and Aled valleys – and of the distant Snowdonia peaks – from the bracken-covered slopes of Mynydd Bodran above Llanfair Talhaiarn.

There are impressive views of Llandudno, along the coast and across the Conwy Estuary to the mountains of Snowdonia on this short circuit of the Great Orme.

An absorbing walk near the Dee Estuary that links a fascinating series of industrial remains with two medieval religious monuments.

Both the old and new castles at Hawarden can be seen, and towards the end comes a walk through delightful woodland bordering Hawarden Park.

A walk that really does have everything: a climb that comes right at the beginning, spectacular scenery, historic attractions and a relaxing finale along a canal towpath.

A varied and most attractive walk that combines a lovely stroll beside the River Conwy with a ramble along the edge of Gwydyr Forest high above the valley.

The first half is mainly through woodland, the second half keeps close to the River Lledr, and there are grand views throughout of Snowdon, Moel Siabod and Dolwyddelan Castle.

This lengthy but easy circuit of Llyn Brenig takes you across heathland and through part of Clocaenog Forest, with views of the moorlands of Mynydd Hiraethog.

On this circuit of Llyn Padarn there are views of Snowdon, attractive woodland, relics of the Llanberis slate quarrying industry, a medieval castle and pleasant walking beside the lake.

This walk around Llyn y Gader lies between the Snowdon and Hebog ranges and there are particularly impressive views of the Nantlle ridge and Yr Aran.

A stiff climb out of Penmaenmawr to the prehistoric Druid's Circle is rewarded by superb views, both along the coast and inland over the Carneddau.

Throughout this highly attractive walk on the Clwydian Hills, mostly on well-defined tracks, the views across the Vale of Clwyd are magnificent.

The views both from the top of Pistyll Rhaeadr and of the waterfall itself are awe-inspiring.

From this most northerly section of the Clwydian range, the views extend over Prestatyn and Rhyl and along the coast to the Great Orme.

Two waterfalls are the main features of this walk through part of the extensive forest of Coed-y-Brenin.

An entirely flat walk across the marshes of the Morfa Rhuddlan that takes you from the mouth of the River Clwyd upstream to the imposing ruins of Rhuddlan Castle.

The summit of Snowdon is the mecca for all serious mountain walkers and this ascent, via the Watkin Path, is one of the most attractive and memorable.

On this circuit of Tal-y-llyn Lake, you enjoy superb and constantly changing views across the water to the surrounding mountains.

The dominating feature of this walk is Telford's majestic Pontcysyllte Aqueduct which carries the Shropshire Union Canal over the Dee Valley.

A beautiful walk, mainly through the extensive woodlands that clothe the sides of the Vale of Ffestiniog.

# Introduction to North Wales, Snowdon and Offa's Dyke

The first title on North Wales in the *Pathfinder®* series of walking guides mainly covered the Snowdonia National Park and also featured some walks in the Lleyn Peninsula and on the Isle of Anglesey. This second title contains some more walks in the National Park, including another ascent of Snowdon itself, but extends eastwards to embrace the less well-known but highly attractive countryside of north-east Wales that lies between Snowdonia and the English border: the Berwyn Mountains, Mynydd Hiraethog, the Clwydian Hills, the Dee Valley and the Vale of Clwyd.

## North-East Wales

This is a region of hills and vales, moorlands and forests, rather than mountains, although the smooth, grassy slopes of the Berwyns rise to over 2,700ft (822m) as they sweep across the area to the east of Bala Lake to descend into the Vale of Llangollen. To the north of Llangollen, beyond the Horseshoe Pass, the broad and fertile Vale of Clwyd stretches to the North Wales holiday coast and the reclaimed marshlands of the Morfa Rhuddlan. To the west the Vale is bordered by the moorlands of Mynydd Hiraethog, partially covered by the conifers of Clocaenog Forest. To the east is the switchback range of the Clwydian Hills, rising to 1,818ft (554m) at Moel Famau and providing a succession of magnificent viewpoints over the Vale. Threading its way across the ridge of the Clwydians is one of the most spectacular sections of Offa's Dyke Path National Trail, which provides opportunities for energetic but highly scenic and enjoyable walking before it descends to the coast at Prestatyn.

To the east of the Clwydians, rolling country leads to the Dee and the English border. In the Middle Ages, Chester, the major town on the River Dee, was the launching pad for successive English invasions of North Wales and the narrow coastal strip was the easiest way in. A whole series of castles line this route, including the first two built by Edward I – at Flint and Rhuddlan – during the course of his successful conquest of Wales in the late 13th century, forerunners of the great castles that surround Snowdonia. Another outstanding castle is the border fortress at Chirk, continually modernised and occupied since it was built.

Apart from the medieval castles, other historic monuments range from prehistoric hillforts to the beautifully situated ruins of Valle Crucis Abbey, and from the cathedral at St Asaph to various industrial remains. The Industrial Revolution has left its mark on parts of north-east Wales, and no visitor can fail to be impressed by Thomas Telford's soaring aqueducts at Pontcysyllte and Chirk, and the series of industrial buildings in the

Greenfield Valley on the Dee Estuary, now a heritage park. At the south end of the valley is a very different monument, the well and chapel of St Winefride at Holywell, the 'Lourdes of Wales'.

*Looking up the River Lledr towards Snowdon (Walk 17)*

## Snowdonia

Here can be found some of the most spectacular scenery in Britain and presiding imperially over this array of jagged ridges and formidable-looking peaks is Yr Wyddfa, the highest mountain in Britain south of the Scottish Highlands. It is known by its more familiar name, allegedly bestowed upon it by Dark Age sailors, who when voyaging from Ireland to Wales saw snow-covered hills on the skyline and christened them the Snowy Hills or 'Snaudune', initially a collective name that later became restricted to the highest peak only.

The Snowdonia mountains can be divided into a number of clearly defined ranges, each with their own characteristics. By far the most popular and most frequently climbed are the Carneddau, the Glyders and Snowdon itself in the north of the region. The great ridges and sweeping grassy slopes of the Carneddau cover an extensive area between the Conwy Valley and the Nant Ffrancon Pass and in the north descend abruptly to the coast. Between the Nant Ffrancon and Llanberis passes rise the majestic Glyders, their shattered volcanic rocks providing the spectacular pinnacles and formations that litter the summits of Glyder Fawr and Glyder Fach. Beyond the Llanberis Pass is Snowdon itself, accessible from a number of routes, and to the west of Snowdon lies the Hebog range.

The central zone of Snowdonia comprises the shapely mass of Moel Siabod between the Llugwy and Lledr valleys, the Moelwyns and Cnicht, the latter sometimes known as the 'Welsh Matterhorn'. Also in the central area are the isolated twin Arenig peaks, the outlines of which can be seen across the featureless expanses of the Migneint, looking towards Bala Lake.

On the other side of Bala Lake the Aran range comprises a long ridge running south-westwards towards the Rhinogs and Cadair Idris, which lie close to the Cardigan Bay coast. The Rhinogs stretch in a long line from Vale of Ffestiniog in the north to the Mawddach Estuary in the south, and

*Water chute near Llyn y Gader (Walk 14)*

to the south of the Mawddach towers the familiar profile of Cadair Idris.

As well as mountain climbs the region has plenty of easy low-level walks. Separating the ranges are delightful valleys, like the steep-sided gorges of the Llugwy and Lledr near Betws-y-Coed and the wider Vale of Ffestiniog. Scattered throughout the area are a number of lakes of varying size. Among the most beautiful of these are Tal-y-llyn and the Cregennan Lakes overlooked by Cadair Idris, Llyn y Gader below the western flanks of Snowdon, Llyn Ogwen dramatically situated between the Glyders and the Carneddau, and Llynnau Mymbyr near Capel Curig, from whose shores there is possibly the finest view of all of Snowdon.

When travelling through Snowdonia the foremost historic remains that catch the eye are the great medieval castles, among the finest in Europe. Some of these were built by the native Welsh princes, as at Dolwyddelan, reputed birthplace of Llewellyn the Great, and Dolbadarn, but most were built by Edward I. In order to consolidate his conquest of Wales, Edward encircled Snowdonia with the formidable and highly expensive castles of Conwy, Beaumaris, Caernarfon and Harlech, all embodying the latest sophistications of castle construction. These castles remain as examples of medieval military architecture at its most advanced and refined.

By far the most striking and large-scale man-made intrusions on the landscape of Snowdonia have come from 19th- and 20th-century industrial and commercial developments. Foremost among these was the slate quarrying industry which reached its peak at the end of the 19th century. It has now largely disappeared but around Llanberis and Blaenau Ffestiniog the remains of that industry have been turned into fascinating tourist attractions.

Later developments include the extensive conifer plantations of Gwydyr, Beddgelert, Coed-y-Brenin and Dyfi forests, the construction of reservoirs and the building of the nuclear power station at Trawsfynnyd. In 1951, as a recognition of its unique landscape value, Snowdonia became one of Britain's first national parks.

### Walking in the area

With its magnificent and varied scenery and wealth of historic attractions, it is not surprising that North Wales is one of the most popular walking destinations in Britain. In the following selection of routes, the aim has been to include all aspects of the landscape of the region and to provide a balance of easy, moderate and more challenging walks. *It must be emphasised that the ascents of Carnedd Dafydd and Snowdon – and some of the other peaks on the Berwyns and Clwydians – should not be undertaken in poor weather conditions, especially in winter, unless you are experienced and properly equipped for such conditions and able to navigate by using a compass.*

So take your pick. At one end of the spectrum is an entirely flat walk beside the River Clwyd from Rhyl to Rhuddlan; at the other is a lengthy and demanding ascent of Snowdon itself. Read carefully the general descriptions of each of the walks, and the distances and approximate times, and choose those which best suit your interests, level of ability and fitness, the amount of time available, and – above all – the state of the weather, and enjoy exploring this wonderful area in the best possible way, on foot.

With the introduction of **'gps enabled' walks,** you will see that this book now includes a list of waypoints alongside the description of the walk. We have included these so that you can enjoy the full benefits of gps should you wish to. Gps is an amazingly useful and entertaining navigational aid, and you do not need to be computer literate to enjoy it.

GPS waypoint co-ordinates add value to your walk. You will now have the extra advantage of introducing 'direction' into your walking which will enhance your leisure walking and make it safer. Use of a gps brings greater confidence and security and you will find you cover ground a lot faster should you need to.

For essential information on map reading and basic navigation, read the *Pathfinder® Guide Map Reading Skills* by outdoor writer, Terry Marsh (ISBN 978-0-7117-4978-8). For more information on using your gps, read the *Pathfinder® Guide GPS for Walkers*, by gps teacher and navigation trainer, Clive Thomas (ISBN 978-0-7117-4445-5). Both titles are available in bookshops or can be ordered online at www.totalwalking.co.uk

*Greenfield Valley Heritage Park*

# Greenfield Valley Heritage Park

| | | GPS waypoints |
|---|---|---|
| **Start** | Greenfield Valley Heritage Park, north end off A548 |  SJ 197 775 |
| **Distance** | 2½ miles (4km) | Ⓐ SJ 196 774 |
| **Approximate time** | 1½ hours | Ⓑ SJ 185 765 |
| **Parking** | Car park at north end of Heritage Park off A548 | Ⓒ SJ 187 766 |
| **Refreshments** | Pub near St Winefride's Well, café in Heritage Park | |
| **Ordnance Survey maps** | Landranger 116 (Denbigh & Colwyn Bay), Explorer 265 (Clwydian Range) | |

*The remains of the former industries of the Greenfield Valley have been incorporated into an imaginative heritage park and provide the basis for a fascinating walk. At either end of the park are examples of the earlier history of the area: the medieval ruins of Basingwerk Abbey, and St Winefride's Well on the edge of Holywell. In addition there is pleasant woodland and attractive views across the Dee Estuary to the Wirral.*

During the 18th and 19th centuries, the Greenfield Valley was a hive of industrial activity, producing textiles and copper and brass goods. The industries have gone and the valley is now peaceful but many of its buildings have fortunately been preserved as the basis for the heritage park, and the former millpools

*The medieval ruins of Basingwerk Abbey*

serve a recreational purpose.

With your back to the road, turn left to the far corner of the car park and take the path that heads uphill.

Ⓐ Just as you reach the ruins of Basingwerk Abbey on your right, turn sharp left on a path, then sharp right to join the embankment of the former Holywell Railway, built in 1869 to transport minerals extracted from local quarries. It closed in 1954 and has been converted into an attractive footpath that runs the length of the valley.

Walk along the track, go through a kissing-gate, cross a bridge and continue along the main track all the while. The various sites that can be seen below through the trees will be visited on the return leg. Remain on this gently rising track for nearly one mile (1.6km), crossing several cross-tracks and paths. At the point where a *circular*

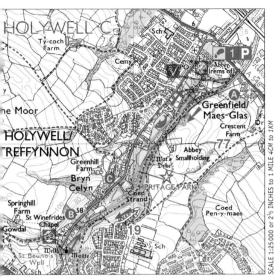

grassy path beside Battery Pool to your right. At the end of the pool turn right to cross a dam – ahead is a chimney and to the left the buildings of Greenfield Mill – and in front of the chimney turn left along a path beside the ruined mill, established in 1776 to shape pots and pans from brass sheets. The path bends left to pass through the fringes of the complex, shortly passing beside the old clock tower to reach a metal kissing-gate at the entrance to a car park. Walk through this car park above Meadow Mill Pool, descend some steps and turn right across another dam at the end of the pool. Once on the other side, turn left downhill, walk through part of the buildings of Meadow Mill, which once produced rolled copper sheets, and continue along the right-hand edge of the larger Flour Mill Pool, joining a tarmac track. Pass above lower Cotton Mill and the site of the Abbey Wire Mill – the latter, now an attractive garden, used to make copper and brass wire. Where the tarmac track curves left around the end of the mill, turn right along a track, passing between the site of the Parys Copper Works on the left, built in 1787, and Abbey Farm Museum on the right.

At a T-junction turn right and pass between the Farm Museum and Visitor Centre on the right and the medieval ruins of Basingwerk Abbey on the left. The mainly 13th-century abbey was founded in 1132 and dissolved by Henry VIII in 1536. Little of the church survives, but substantial remains of the cloisters and domestic buildings can still be seen.

After passing the abbey, follow the track to the left and descend steps Ⓐ to return to the car park. ●

SCALE 1:25000 or 2½ INCHES to 1 MILE 4CM to 1KM

brick mill chimney is visible close-by on your right, fork right on a lesser path, shortly passing through a metal kissing-gate beside a barrier. Bend right through a parking area between factories to reach the main valley road.

Ⓑ Turn left to St Winefride's Well and Chapel, the 'Lourdes of Wales'. According to legend, Winefride, a 7th-century maiden, had her head cut off for spurning the advances of a local noble. Where the head fell, a spring gushed out of the ground, the origin of the holy well that gives its name to the nearby town. Miraculously, the head was later reunited with the rest of Winefride and she became an abbess. In the Middle Ages the well was alleged to have healing powers and became one of the principal shrines in the country. It was enclosed by the elaborate chapel in the late 15th century by Lady Margaret Beaufort, mother of Henry VII.

Retrace your steps along the road, remaining on this to reach the Royal Oak pub on your right. Ⓒ At the entrance to the pub's car park, take the hand-railed path on the left, dropping to walk a

# Great Orme

| Start | Great Orme Country Park, signposted from centre of Llandudno. Alternatively come on either the Cabin Lift or Tramway from Llandudno |
|---|---|
| Distance | 3½ miles (5.6km) |
| Approximate time | 2 hours |
| Parking | Great Orme Country Park |
| Refreshments | Hotel and restaurant at Great Orme Country Park |
| Ordnance Survey maps | Landranger 115 (Snowdon), Explorer OL17 (Snowdon – Conwy Valley) |

**GPS waypoints**

🖉 SH 765 833
Ⓐ SH 774 829
Ⓑ SH 770 838
Ⓒ SH 757 840

*The familiar and distinctive headland of the Great Orme rises to 679ft (207m) above the elegant resort of Llandudno and its summit, from where the walk starts, can be reached by chairlift and tramway from the town centre as well as by car. Most of it is now a country park and on this short circuit there is a succession of outstanding views that take in Llandudno and its curving bay, the Conwy Estuary, mountains of Snowdonia, the Menai Strait and the island of Anglesey. Historic interest is provided by the Great Orme Mines and St Tudno's Church.*

As well as the superb views, attractions on the Great Orme range from Bronze Age copper mines and a Dark Age Christian site to the Edwardian tramway, first opened in 1902, and modern chairlift and dry ski-slope.

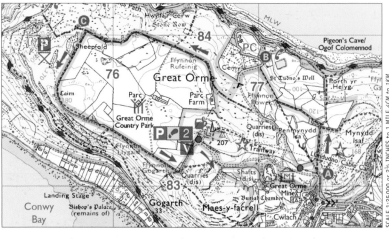

SCALE 1:25000 or 2½ INCHES to 1 MILE 4CM to 1KM

```
0    200   400   600   800 METRES  1
0    200   400   600   800  1000 YARDS
                                        KILOMETRES
                                        MILES
                                        1
```

*St Tudno's Church*

Retrace your steps to the Visitor Centre and turn down the road, tramway on your left. Join the grassy path to the right of the road; as the road bends left this path continues down alongside a wall (marked by low marker posts with a white 'walker' on), shortly passing a Great Orme Historical Trail Information Board. At a fingerpost amidst bracken, keep right to drop to a tarred lane just above the Great Orme Mines. These are old copper mines, first worked in at least 1580BC and as such the oldest known metal-working site in Britain. Turn right, ignore the left fork to the mine and shortly bend left along the roughening track that passes above the Visitor Centre. Remain on this track through a metal gate and past houses. Go ahead on the tarred lane and bear left to reach a junction at St Beunos Road and the main road carrying the steep tram tracks.

**Ⓐ** Turn left uphill, go through the gate beside a cattle-grid and then turn right, cross the tramway and walk along the rough lane signed as a footpath for St Tudno's Church. At the fork in 50 paces keep right on the gravel lane, walking through to a turning area at Pink Farm. Look right here for a kissing-gate and multiple fingerposts, go through this and turn left. Pass through a metal gate virtually behind the farm and cottage and go ahead along a fenced track. Passing a field gate, this narrows to a path; go through two kissing-gates and keep ahead to reach a lane and St Tudno's Church.

**Ⓑ** Turn uphill and wind with the road above the sloping graveyards. About 50 yds (46m) beyond the upper boundary wall, fork right through some roadside boulders onto a wide grassy path through bracken. This cuts through to a sheep-cropped grass common; bear right up across this to find a gravel lane and turn right, shortly picking up a stone estate wall on your left. This is your constant companion for the remainder of the walk. There are excellent views across the Irish Sea; on very clear days the Isle of Man and the Lake District's mountains can be seen.

**Ⓒ** At a wall corner turn left, continue beside it and follow it as it curves left again. Now come possibly the finest views of the walk, looking across the Conwy Estuary to Conwy town and castle, with the panorama of the Snowdonia mountains visible on the horizon.

Keep beside the wall where it turns left again and head uphill to return to the start. ●

# *Caergwrle and Hope*

| | | GPS waypoints |
|---|---|---|
| **Start** | Caergwrle | 🖊 SJ 305 574 |
| **Distance** | 4 miles (6.4km) | Ⓐ SJ 311 576 |
| **Approximate time** | 2 hours | Ⓑ SJ 310 583 |
| **Parking** | Caergwrle | Ⓒ SJ 321 587 |
| **Refreshments** | Pubs at Caergwrle, pubs at Hope | Ⓓ SJ 324 585 |
| **Ordnance Survey maps** | Landranger 117 (Chester & Wrexham), Explorer 256 (Wrexham) | Ⓔ SJ 318 576 |

*Towards the end of this pleasant and easy paced walk in the Alyn Valley, there are fine views of the wooded slopes of Hope Mountain. On such a modest walk there should be enough energy at the end for a climb to the ruins of Caergwrle Castle, a grand viewpoint.*

In the 19th century Caergwrle was a spa town and visitors used to come here to take the waters prior to a walk up Hope Mountain.

🖊 Begin by turning left out of the car park along High Street and take the first turning on the right, passing to the right of a church. Follow a narrow lane to a road, cross over and continue along a tarmac track which descends to cross a 17th-century packhorse bridge over the River Alyn. Head uphill between houses and cottages, cross a railway line and descend to a road.

Walk ahead up the concrete drive opposite. Near the top, look on your right for steps up to a stile, climb this and turn left. Walk outside the property boundary to another stile in a cross-fence ahead. Climb this and turn left along a fenced path. Ⓐ Remain on this path which shortly skirts a line of trees. This is the line of Wat's Dyke. Like the better-known and more extensive Offa's Dyke, this was constructed in the 8th or 9th century as a boundary between the Kingdom of Mercia and the Welsh.

Climb a stile and remain with the fenced path, rising beside a driveway to a road. Turn left, take the first turning on the left and follow a lane up to Hope church. In front of the medieval church turn right Ⓑ along a track to the road, cross over and take the tarmac track opposite. Just after passing a farm, turn left, at a public footpath sign, descend to a stile, climb it and bear right to head diagonally uphill across a field. Descend to climb another stile and turn right along the right edge of two fields, climbing two stiles. After a third stile keep along the left edge of the field, turn right in the corner and look for another stile on your left. Climb this and go ahead to a further stile into a grassy track. Keep ahead past a cottage to a lane.

Ⓒ Turn right along this and after ¹⁄₄ mile (400m) – just after passing a large brick house on the left – turn right over a stile Ⓓ and walk across a field to a metal gate. Go through, continue across the next field, climb a stile and keep ahead to join and keep alongside the left field edge. Go through a gate near the field corner, head diagonally across the next field and descend to go through a gate. Walk the track past ruins and through another gate. As the track turns left, look carefully on your right for a curious stile across sheathed barbed wire hidden in overgrown bushes. Walk along the right edge of the pasture to a point 30 paces beyond the second pylon; here fork half-left up the bank, pass through the line of old hedge and continue half-right to an unusual three-way stile in the field corner. Bear right along the lane to reach a T-junction.

**E** Cross the main road and climb the stile opposite. Walk along the right-hand edge of a field, pass through a hedge gap and keep ahead to the edge of the wooded hill of Caer Estyn, the site of an Iron Age hill-fort. Turn right, climb two stiles in quick succession and keep along the left edge of a field below the wooded hill. Climb a stile, cross the quarry road and take another stile into a fenced path that continues to skirt the foot of Caer Estyn. This gradually descends the field edge, with good views ahead across Caergwrle and the Alyn Valley to Hope Mountain, right to Hope church and the distant industrial complexes of Deeside.

The path drops to reach the stile near to point **A** and used earlier in the walk. Cross the stile and walk down alongside the boundary fence ahead to find the steps down onto the concrete drive. Walk down to the road and turn left. Go across the river bridge beside the pub and cross carefully to the right. Go under the railway bridge and turn right along Castle Street. Stay on this to the T-junction with High Street. Here turn right to return to the car park. A short diversion to the left, however brings you to a path on the left beside the war memorial, which rises steeply to Caergwrle Castle, a superb viewpoint. The meagre remains are of a late 12th-century castle originally built by Dafydd ap Gruffyd, the brother of Llewellyn ap Gruffyd who was the last independent Prince of Wales. It was later rebuilt by Edward I after his successful Welsh campaigns but abandoned shortly afterwards.

Descend from the castle and walk along High Street back to the start.  ●

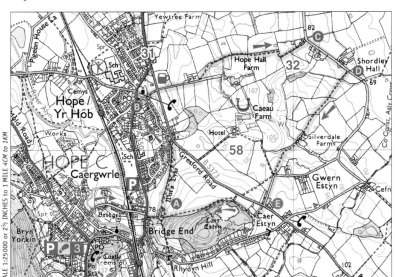

# *Rhyl and Rhuddlan*

| | | GPS waypoints |
|---|---|---|
| **Start** | Rhyl, Foryd Bridge at west end of promenade | 🖊 SH 996 806 |
| | | Ⓐ SH 994 806 |
| **Distance** | 5½ miles (8.75km) | Ⓑ SJ 020 778 |
| **Approximate time** | 2½ hours | Ⓒ SJ 022 780 |
| **Parking** | Rhyl, near Foryd Bridge | Ⓓ SJ 002 806 |
| **Refreshments** | Pubs and cafés at Rhyl, pubs and cafés at Rhuddlan | |
| **Ordnance Survey maps** | Landranger 116 (Denbigh & Colwyn Bay), Explorer 264 (Vale of Clwyd) | |

*This fresh, easy and wholly flat walk follows the west bank of the River Clwyd from its estuary at Rhyl Harbour to Rhuddlan Castle, and returns along its east bank. From the raised embankments above the river marshes there are open and extensive views across the marsh (Morfa Rhuddlan) to the surrounding hills.*

Rhyl is one of the most popular holiday resorts on the North Wales coast with every conceivable type of entertainment. Of Victorian origin, it has developed a number of new amenities in recent years, including an indoor Sun Centre, and also has a fine sandy beach.

🖊 The walk begins at the Foryd Bridge over the River Clwyd. Cross the bridge and take the first turning on the left Ⓐ. The lane soon becomes a rough track. Immediately after passing under a railway bridge, turn left up to a stile. Climb it and continue along a grassy embankment above the marshland and grassland beside the Clwyd. All the way there are fine views across the marsh, the Morfa Rhuddlan, to the line of the Clwydian Hills. Among the landmarks in sight are the spire of the Marble Church at Bodelwyddan to the right, the tower of St Asaph Cathedral in front, and the walls of Rhuddlan Castle to the left. Cross a footbridge over the little River Gele, continue along the track

which after the next stile becomes a straight, tarmac track, pass under a road bridge and keep ahead to a road Ⓑ. Turn left and cross a bridge over the river into Rhuddlan. To the right is the imposing late 13th-century castle, one of a chain built by Edward I to consolidate his control of North Wales. In order to make it accessible from the sea, the King had the River Clwyd straightened and deepened and Rhuddlan became an important port. A short way beyond the castle is the only remaining part of its Norman predecessor, a mound called Twthill, built by William the Conqueror in 1073. The Old Parliament House in High Street is alleged to be where Edward I enacted the Statute of Rhuddlan in 1284. As a result of this, Wales was brought fully under English administration and divided up into counties on the English pattern.

Immediately after crossing the bridge, turn left Ⓒ along a lane which passes

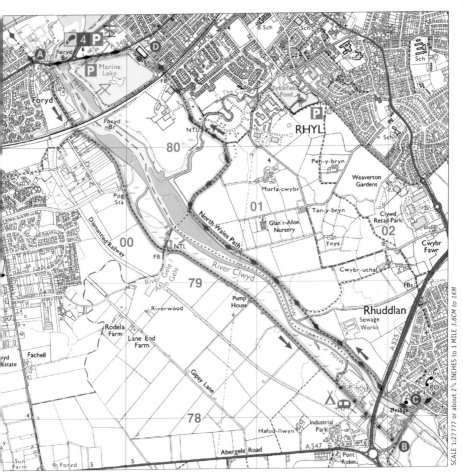

SCALE 1:27 777 or about 2¼ INCHES to 1 MILE 3.6CM to 1KM

| | | | | | | | |
|---|---|---|---|---|---|---|---|
| 0 | 200 | 400 | 600 | 800 METRES | 1 | | |
| 0 | 200 | 400 | 600 YARDS | ½ | KILOMETRES MILES | | |

in front of the mainly 15th-century church. This has a double nave, a characteristic of many of the churches of the Vale of Clwyd. At a sharp right-hand bend, fork left along the gravelly lane. Just after a redundant cattle-grid rise left up a path to gain the embankment and turn right to pass beneath the concrete road bridge. Remain on this wildflower-rich embankment for well over a mile, passing through several gate-stiles. The River Clwyd here is rich with water birds – look out for the innumerable cormorants and shags spreading their wings to dry them off.

The path eventually reaches the start of a high wire fence on your left. Remain beside this, leaving the river behind. Simply trace the line of the fence, cross an access track and soon bend left to pass to the left of a large residential caravan site here at the edge of Rhyl. Occasional North Wales Path discs confirm the route. Ignore a finger-posted turn right. The path becomes surfaced before reaching the end of the site; go through a kissing-gate and turn left along the tarred lane serving garages. Use the footbridge over the coastal rail-way and take the second turn on the left.

**D** This is signed as a cycleway and leads to the shore of Rhyl Marine Lake, opened in 1895 as part of a pleasure park. Bear right to walk around the shoreline to return to the start near Foryd Bridge. ●

Denbigh and the Ystrad Valley

# Denbigh and the Ystrad Valley

| Start | Denbigh | | GPS waypoints |
|---|---|---|---|
| Distance | 5 miles (8km) | | 🖊 SJ 050 661 |
| Approximate time | 2½ hours | | Ⓐ SJ 050 656 |
| Parking | Denbigh | | Ⓑ SJ 057 649 |
| Refreshments | Pubs and cafés at Denbigh | | Ⓒ SJ 054 649 |
| Ordnance Survey maps | Landranger 116 (Denbigh & Colwyn Bay), Explorer 264 (Vale of Clwyd) | | Ⓓ SJ 044 652 |
| | | | Ⓔ SJ 032 650 |
| | | | Ⓕ SJ 049 657 |

*Although a short walk, this route is full of interest and provides a succession of outstanding views across the Vale of Clwyd. From Denbigh you descend into the valley of the little River Ystrad and follow its course, across meadows and through woodland, to the ruins of a small cottage associated with Dr Johnson. Near the end comes a dramatic view of Denbigh Castle, perched on its hill above the town and Vale with the long line of the Clwydian range on the horizon.*

The walled town of Denbigh is dominated by the ruins of its late-13th-century castle. It was built by the powerful Henry de Lacy, Earl of Lincoln, who was entrusted by Edward I with the task of keeping the local area firmly under English control. Apart from its extent, the most impressive feature of the castle is the elaborate three-towered gateway. Most of the town walls, contemporary with the castle, survive, though the modern town has moved down the hill outside them. Within the walls are the remains of two churches. The first is the shell of an Elizabethan cathedral, 'Leicester's Church', intended by Robert Dudley, Earl of Leicester and Lord of Denbigh, to replace the cathedral at St Asaph but never completed. The second is a surviving tower from the medieval town chapel of St Hilary.

🖊 The walk begins in the town centre, facing the Library and Museum Gallery. Pass to the right of it, turn right steeply up Bull Lane, go round a right bend and continue up St Hilary's Terrace, passing Leicester's Church. Turn right, then left, passing the tower of St Hilary's Church, and then right again in front of the castle. At a T-junction, turn left below the castle walls, head down to another T-junction and turn left.

Ⓐ At a public footpath sign turn left along an enclosed track which later narrows to a hedge-lined path. The path descends but before reaching the bottom, turn right through a metal kissing-gate and walk along the fenced path to use a second kissing-gate. From here head half-left, gently downhill across the sloping pasture to the bottom corner and a stile and kissing-gate. Use the stile, put the hedge on your left and walk to and through another kissing-gate; keep the hedge left to reach several gateways at a corner. Go straight on, putting a hedge on your right, and walk on to a stile. Climb this and hug the top of the field to another stile in a corner.

**B** Climb this stile and walk along the wooded path, an occasionally very narrow passage. Climb two stiles before eventually reaching a lane. Turn right, uphill and walk to find a finger-posted track on your left beside a copse.

**C** Turn along this and remain on it, eventually passing in front of a remote house. Beyond here the track shrinks to a wide woodland path, shortly passing through a handgate. Remain on this peaceful path just above the River Ystrad to reach an old gate blocking the way. Fork left here, climb the nearby stile and walk the left side of the riverside meadow. Climb another stile and keep ahead, joining the green hollow to the right of a distinct mound. Go through a field gate and ahead past

the cottage to a corner stile. Climb this and turn right up the lane.

**D** In 200 yds (182m) double back-left along a grassy, hedged track. This passes behind a range of estate buildings before becoming a wooded path. Climb a stile beside a gate to enter a long riverside meadow – on your right is the tree-shrouded ruin of Dr Johnson's Cottage, said to be where the renowned traveller and lexicographer stayed during a tour of Wales. At the end of the meadow climb the stile into the woods and immediately fork right up a steep path to the top edge of the trees.

**E** Climb the stile and turn right up beside the woods; the field funnels into a long entry and another stile. Climb this and bend left (*N.B. – not the stile into more woods*) on a field track that leads to a gateway. Go through this and walk ahead to a stone and slate stile at a

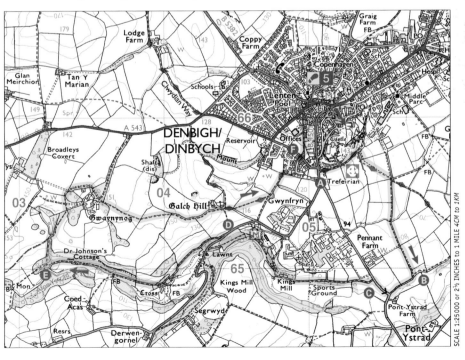

*Denbigh and Denbigh Castle*

wooded corner. Take this and keep right to a farther stile; once over this bend right along the edge of the large field outside the estate wall. Use another stile beside a gate on your right and keep ahead along the dirt road. Cross straight over the driveway to the imposing Gwaynynog Manor (where Beatrix Potter worked on illustrations for her books) and walk on with the field road, grand views of the Clwydian range drawing the eye ahead.

Climb a stile and head a hair's breadth left, aiming for a stile beneath an oak in the far field boundary. From here are excellent views across to Denbigh Castle. Walk along the left side of the field (ignore the stile in 20 paces) to use another stile in 100 yds (91m). Keep to the left of this field to drop to a stile on the left near a cottage. Climb

this and turn right down the grassy track beside the cottage, shortly joining a rough lane. *(N.B. – in summer 2005 some minor path diversions were planned here, but changes are minimal and mostly involve new stiles to avoid using the grassy track. Look for waymarking.)* Stay on this lane for about 120 yds (110m) to a finger-posted stone stile on your left. Climb this and walk diagonally right to the far corner and a stone stile beside a gateway (Clwydian Way disc here). Use this and trace the right side of the field to take a stile into an enclosed path behind housing.

This bends left to emerge on an estate road. Turn left to reach a T-junction. **F** Turn right and immediately cross the road to join a tarred path on the left dropping past allotment gardens. Keep ahead on the lane at the bottom to reach a junction. Turn right to return to the centre of Denbigh. ●

# Hawarden Park

| Start | Hawarden | GPS waypoints | |
|---|---|---|---|
| Distance | 5½ miles (8.9km) | | SJ 316 657 |
| Approximate time | 2½ hours | Ⓐ | SJ 317 657 |
| | | Ⓑ | SJ 326 662 |
| Parking | Hawarden, Tinkersdale car park | Ⓒ | SJ 331 656 |
| Refreshments | Pubs at Hawarden, pub at Old | Ⓓ | SJ 325 653 |
| | Warren | Ⓔ | SJ 329 648 |
| Ordnance Survey maps | Landranger 117 (Chester & | Ⓕ | SJ 328 634 |
| | Wrexham), Explorer 266 (Wirral & | Ⓖ | SJ 321 634 |
| | Chester) | | |

*From many parts of this easy and attractive walk, close to the English border, there are fine views of Deeside and across Hawarden Park to the ruins of the medieval 'Old Castle' and its successor, the 'New Castle', once the home of the great Victorian statesman William Gladstone. Much of the last part of the route runs through the delightful Bilberry Wood alongside the wall of the park.*

Turn right out of the car park and at a crossroads in the village centre, turn right along Glynne Way. Take the first lane on the left, Cross Tree Lane, and at a public footpath sign, turn right Ⓐ on to a path, between a wall on the right and a wire fence on the left, that runs along the edge of school grounds. Ahead are views over Deeside.

Where the fence on the left ends, keep ahead beside a hedge on your right. Where this fails, keep ahead on the walked path beside the remains of a hedge on your left. As this curves left, cut half-right across the rough pasture to find a derelict stile at the corner of hedges (there's a 'Circular Walk' disc here). Use this and turn left alongside the hedge (left) to reach the nearby farmyard. Turn right along the access road to reach a lane. Turn left and at a public footpath sign turn right Ⓑ over a stile into a hedged track. At the end, take the stile beside a small ford and

keep ahead, putting the hedge on your right. Climb a stile into a small grove of cherry trees and keep right to another stile in 30 paces. Take this and turn immediately right (beware the deep ditch ahead) on a narrow path to another nearby stile. Once over this turn left along the field edge. To the right are fine views of both the medieval Hawarden Castle and its later successor. In the frequent wars between English and Welsh, Hawarden occupied a key position on the border and Edward I used the castle as a springboard for his invasion of Wales. Briefly captured by the Welsh under Dafydd ap Gruffyd in 1282, it was soon recovered by the English and Dafydd was killed the following year. It fell into ruin after the Civil War between Charles I and Parliament. The 'New Castle' was built in 1752 and became the home of William Gladstone in 1852 after his marriage to Catherine Glynne. He lived there until his death in 1898.

Climb a stile, keep ahead, climb another one and turn right **C** along a lane to a T-junction **D**. Turn left along a road for nearly $^1/_2$ mile (800m) and at a public footpath sign, turn right **E** over a stile and walk across a field to climb another one on the far side. Follow a path, waymarked with yellow-topped posts, through young conifers to a stile, climb it and continue through trees to another stile. Climb this and turn left with the waymarks, following these down through conifers and over a cross track to cross a footbridge. Pass

just right of the large oak tree and walk up the rise, aiming for a stile left of the farthest visible wooden pylon.

Climb the stile, turn right along the tarmac lane and after passing to the left of a farm and going through a metal gate, it becomes a rough track. Continue along this wide, hedge-lined track, climbing a stile, to a lane and turn right **F** through the hamlet of Old Warren. At a public footpath sign at the edge of trees, turn right **G** on to the lane to Cherry Orchard Farm, climb a stile and continue along this straight road which later curves left towards Bilberry Wood. On this part of the walk are more fine views of both castles.

*The woodland path beside Hawarden Park*

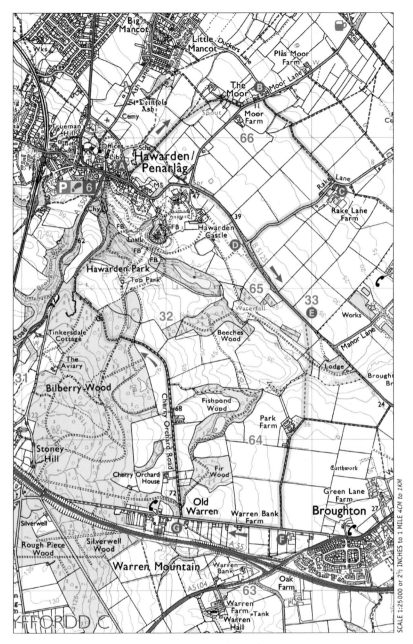

Climb a stile into the woods and go ahead on the forest road. In 100 yds (91m) keep left at the fork, then bear right as waymarked, continuing along the grassy forest road. This eventually joins the line of the estate wall on your right. Climb one stile, and stay beside the wall to a second, ruinous stile. Bear

left from here to a third stile near a gate leading into a wide old track. Cross the culvert and pass above the ruined mill, then fork right alongside the handrail to rise to the car park. ●

# Pistyll Rhaeadr

| | | GPS waypoints |
|---|---|---|
| **Start** | Tan-y-pistyll, at end of minor road 4 miles (6.4km) north-west of Llanrhaeadr-ym-Mochnant | ⬩ SJ 074 294<br>Ⓐ SJ 072 295<br>Ⓑ SJ 085 287 |
| **Distance** | 3 miles (4.8km) | |
| **Approximate time** | 1½ hours | |
| **Parking** | Tan-y-pistyll | |
| **Refreshments** | Farm café (seasonal) at Tan-y-pistyll | |
| **Ordnance Survey maps** | Landranger 125 (Bala & Lake Vyrnwy), Explorer 255 (Llangollen & Berwyn) | |

*Initially you climb up to a magnificent viewpoint at the top of Pistyll Rhaeadr, the highest waterfall in Wales, overlooking the Rhaeadr Valley and the surrounding slopes of the Berwyn Mountains. After the descent, the route continues along a lane through the valley and returns to the start via tracks and fieldpaths close to the river. At the end comes a dramatic view of the great cascade, one of the 'Seven Wonders of Wales'.*

*Waterfall at Pistyll Rhaeadr*

At the entrance to the car park take the path through a wall gap on your left; remain on it and generally keep right to wind up through the woods to a handgate. Just beyond this, fork left at the fingerpost 'Top of Falls' onto a steeper path up the crag. At a low waymark post at a T-junction turn left on an easier path that rises to a waymark post; here fork left down to a handgate into woods, beyond which a path drops to the top of the falls Ⓐ.

*Take extreme care here as the edge is unfenced and the rocks may be slippery.*

Retrace your steps down to the car park entrance and turn left along the lane. After almost one mile (1.6km) – at the second farm on the right – turn sharp right at a bridleway fingerpost Ⓑ and walk through the farmyard to and through a gate left of barns. Continue along the track which curves left to cross a bridge over the River Rhaeadr and bears right to another farm. After entering the farmyard, bear right with the blue bridleway discs to enter a fenced track leading away from the farm. Go through the gate at the end and bear left along the uppermost track. In 100 yds (91m) fork right onto a narrow level path, shortly passing a waymark post. Continue past a second post amid these lead mine ruins to pick up a path alongside a fence (and cupressus trees) on your right. Remain on this for about 300 yds (274m) to find a stile on the right. Take this and drop to another stile, ford the stream and go ahead with the fence/wall on your right. At a waymarked fork keep left, rising gently over a low rise before following the path ahead into the woods. You'll reach a footbridge here at the foot of Pistyll Rhaeadr; cross this and walk to the car park. ●

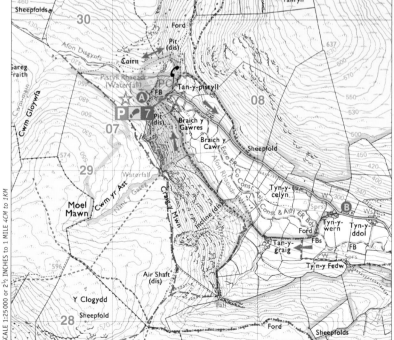

SCALE 1:25 000 or 2½ INCHES to 1 MILE 4CM to 1KM

# Capel Curig

| | | | |
|---|---|---|---|
| **Start** | Capel Curig National Park car park, at west end of village near junction of A5 and A4086 | | **GPS waypoints** |
| **Distance** | 4½ miles (7.2km) | | ✐ SH 720 582 |
| **Approximate time** | 2½ hours | | Ⓐ SH 731 581 |
| **Parking** | Capel Curig | | Ⓑ SH 732 575 |
| **Refreshments** | Pubs and cafés at Capel Curig | | Ⓒ SH 734 571 |
| **Ordnance Survey maps** | Landranger 115 (Snowdon), Explorer OL17 (Snowdon – Conwy Valley) | | Ⓓ SH 731 575 |
| | | | Ⓔ SH 714 578 |
| | | | Ⓕ SH 720 585 |

*This relatively short and undemanding route around Capel Curig has fine views over the surrounding mountains and valleys, areas of woodland, and attractive riverside and lakeside walking. The highlight of the walk, given clear conditions, is the view of Snowdon across Llynnau Mymbyr, one of the great classic views of North Wales.*

Capel Curig is strung out for over 1½ miles (2.4km) along the A5. Situated in the heart of some of the grandest mountain terrain in Snowdonia and with plenty of hotels, guest houses, pubs and cafés, it is a Mecca for walkers, climbers and cyclists. Just to the west of the village is Plas y Brenin, the National Centre for Mountain Activities.

✐ Begin by turning left out of the car park down to the road junction and climb a ladder-stile to the left of the war memorial and half-hidden, 19th-century, Norman-style church. A well-constructed rocky path leads uphill across a field to a wall-gap. Cross the slab bridge beyond and bear right at the fork, soon joining a stone causeway across this marshy pasture to reach a ladder-stile into woodland.

Climb it and walk the woodland path, keeping right at a fork. The path undulates out of the trees and across a bracken-covered slope below Clogwyn-mawr, revealing views, right, across the Llugwy Valley to shapely Moel Siabod. Climb the left one of three ladder-stiles at a fenced corner and rise alongside a fence (right) across slabby pasture for about 500 yds (457m) to reach a small concrete footbridge across a culverted stream.

Ⓐ Do not cross this; instead turn sharp-right and walk alongside the stream, left, then a fence, to cross a slab-bridge. Pick up the line of a property wall/fence on your left, descending to climb a ladder-stile. Bend left to take a gate into a rough lane at a bend. Walk to your left for about 30 paces and then fork left off the track onto a grassy path rising beside a fence, curving round to another ladder-stile. Climb it, later cross a track and descend to climb another ladder-stile into woodland. Continue downhill through this most attractive wood and take the right-hand path at a fork, descending quite steeply, following it around right- and left-hand bends to reach a ladder-

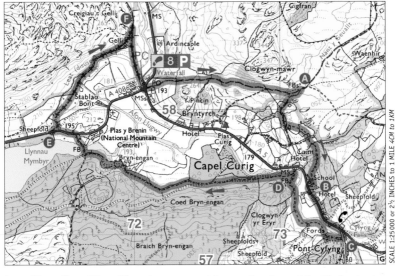

SCALE 1:25000 or 2½ INCHES to 1 MILE 4CM to 1KM

stile to the left of a school **B**.

Climb this stile, turn left along the A5, passing the Tyn y Coed Hotel, and take the first turning on the right. Cross the bridge over the River Llugwy and immediately turn right **C** on to a track. Go through a gate and in a few paces fork right down the wide track, passing below a cottage. The path bends right and crosses a footbridge; from here head half-left to pass to the right of the old stone barn. Now remain on a riverside path heading upstream. Climb a ladder-stile into woodland and walk ahead to take the right-hand of two gaps through a line of rocks. Beyond, rise gently with the path to a junction in front of the snout of a rock face. Fork right and wind with this riverside path through to a constriction above a sharp left-bend in the river.

**D** Immediately around the corner here is Cobden's Footbridge across the Afon Llugwy. Do not cross this but, rather, turn sharp left up a path to reach a fingerpost at a fork. Bear right here, the braided path rising gradually through the woods. Favour your right hand to pick up a singular path beside fencing above a steep drop and old lead mine; the river is far below. Descend some steps and remain on the wide forestry track as it meanders through the superb Coed Bryn-engan woods.

At a major junction bear left for 50 paces and then fork right downhill, the compacted forestry road soon levels and you remain on this to and through a gate above remote houses, shortly thereafter reaching a path junction above the footbridge near to Plas y Brenin National Mountain Centre. Cross this and walk beside the boundary wall. To your left is one of the classic low-level views in Snowdonia, across Llynnau Mymbyr to the majestic Snowdon Horseshoe. Climb a ladder-stile onto the main road and turn left.

**E** As the road bends left, cross to the right and climb a ladder-stile, keep ahead along the rough field road and, at a fork, keep ahead-left, continuing along this track as it gradually bends right and passes through two metal gates. Pass beside the cottage and walk to the nearby ruined barn. **F** Turn sharp right here on another track, climb a ladder-stile and walk the tarred lane back to the start. ●

# Tal-y-llyn Lake

| | | GPS waypoints |
|---|---|---|
| **Start** | Tal-y-llyn | 🗺 SH 714 094 |
| **Distance** | 3½ miles (5.6km) | Ⓐ SH 710 096 |
| **Approximate time** | 2 hours | Ⓑ SH 705 093 |
| **Parking** | Several lay-bys at west end of lake near Ty'n-y-cornel Hotel | Ⓒ SH 709 100 |
| | | Ⓓ SH 722 106 |
| **Refreshments** | Pubs at Tal-y-llyn | Ⓔ SH 728 104 |
| **Ordnance Survey maps** | Landranger 124 (Porthmadog & Dolgellau), Explorer OL23 (Cadair Idris & Llyn Tegid) | |

*Tal-y-llyn Lake, hemmed in by sweeping mountainsides and sheltering below the southern slopes of Cadair Idris, is an outstandingly beautiful lake, as this circuit of it demonstrates. There are glorious and constantly changing views across it throughout the walk, but perhaps the finest are from the north side, where the path climbs up through woodland and then contours above the lake before descending to its low-lying eastern shores. The only climb – a steady and relatively short one – comes near the beginning.*

🗺 Start near the Ty'n-y-cornel Hotel and walk along the road, with the lake on your right, towards the Pen-y-bont Hotel. Opposite the latter is the small, simple but appealing late 15th-century church of St Mary, noted for its fine timber roof. Turn right along a tarmac drive in front of the hotel and just before the drive curves right, turn left through a gate, at a public bridleway sign Ⓐ.

Head uphill along the left inside edge of sloping woodland and at a fork take the right-hand uphill track to a T-junction. Ⓑ Turn sharp right and walk up the steepening path; at the next fork keep right, rising steadily through the woods. Cross diagonally over the old forestry road and trace the narrower path to the edge of the woods. Bear right through a gate beside a cattle-grid, continue more gently uphill along a broad track and where the track bends

left to a farm, keep ahead to ford a stream and climb a ladder-stile.

Keep ahead to a footpath post, bear left to a ladder-stile and, despite the multitude of waymarks, do not climb it but turn right Ⓒ along a gently descending track, by a wire fence and hedge on the left. From this section are probably the finest of many fine views across Tal-y-llyn Lake to the encircling mountains. Go through the farther of two metal field gates and walk beside the fence at the top of the woods. As the trees fail, keep ahead on the track to the far side of the steep pasture and here turn downhill. Walk the woodland edge to find an in-field waymark post pointing the way left to and through a waymarked gate into the trees.

Cross the footbridge and turn right through a wooden gate, then follow the fenced path, then rough track, behind

*View across Tal-y-llyn Lake*

the farmhouse and down to a tarred lane near the barns. Turn left, go through a metal gate and walk along this pleasantly tree-lined track as far as a public footpath sign where you bear right on to a sunken path ⓓ. Bear right again to cross a footbridge over a stream, and then head half-left, diagonally across the reedy meadows at the head of the lake – these will be very soggy in wet weather – to a small metal handgate. Use this, cross the footbridge and head half-left again, using yellow-topped posts to aid navigation to a stile. Cross this and the footbridge and then look slightly left to spot a waymarked gate in the far banked hedge. Go through this and walk beside a double fence on your right. At a fingerposted footbridge, turn right, climb the stile and head across the small pasture to another stile leading directly onto the road.

ⓔ Turn right and follow the lakeside road back to the lay-by some 1¼ miles (2.8km) away. ●

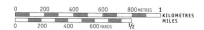

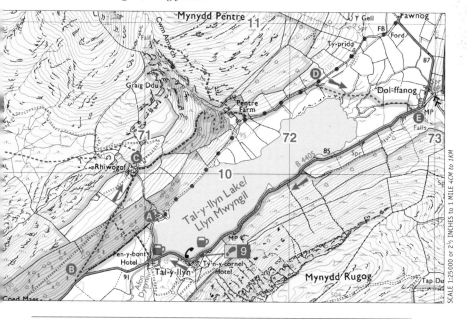

# Cregennen Lakes and Arthog Waterfalls

| | | GPS waypoints |
|---|---|---|
| **Start** | Cregennen Lakes, National Trust car park | SH 657 143 |
| **Distance** | 4 miles (6.5km). Shorter version 3 miles (4.8km) | Ⓐ SH 663 136<br>Ⓑ SH 657 133 |
| **Approximate time** | 2½ hours (1½ hours for shorter walk) | Ⓒ SH 651 140<br>Ⓓ SH 646 144 |
| **Parking** | Cregennen Lakes | Ⓔ SH 655 146 |
| **Refreshments** | None | |
| **Ordnance Survey maps** | Landranger 124 (Porthmadog & Dolgellau), Explorer OL23 (Cadair Idris & Llyn Tegid) | |

*The Cregennen Lakes (Llynnau Cregennen) lie in a lonely and austere setting above the estuary of the River Mawddach and below Cadair Idris, cradled by mountains and accessible only by steep, narrow, twisting lanes. This short walk explores this hauntingly beautiful setting and at several points there are magnificent views over the Mawddach Estuary. There is also the opportunity to view the Arthog Waterfalls, where the Afon Arthog plunges down a wooded ravine in a series of impressive falls. The shorter walk omits the falls.*

*Clapper bridge and Tyrau Mawr*

From the car park turn right along the lane beside one of the lakes and immediately there is a fine view to the left looking towards the northern flanks of Cadair Idris. Follow the lane around several bends and through a metal gate, passing a standing stone, to a T-junction Ⓐ. Turn right, pass a ruined farmhouse and just before the lane reaches a metal gate, turn right Ⓑ through a gate and walk along a grassy path to a

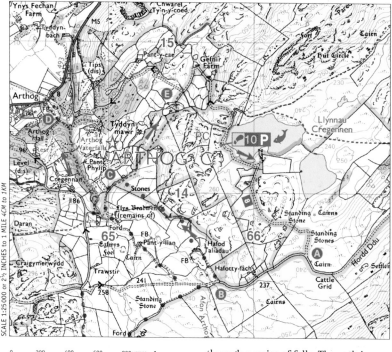

ladder-stile. Climb it and keep ahead, by a wall on the left, going through a metal gate (ignore the fingerpost pointing right) into a funnel-like walled field end. Keep beside the wall on your left to reach a corner and two gates. Ignore these and turn right, putting a wall on your left and pass through two more metal gates to reach a T-junction of tracks at a footpath post **C**.

*For the shorter walk, turn right here and follow the directions from* **C** *below.* For the eminently worthwhile detour to the Arthog Waterfalls, turn left along a walled track to a metal gate. Go through this and remain on the track for about 150 yds (137m), then look right for a clapper bridge across the little Afon Arthog. Cross this and turn right onto a track. Almost immediately bear right and climb a ladder-stile to enter a wooded ravine. Continue along a delightful path that descends this ravine beside the river which cascades down

through a series of falls. The path is winding and steep in places, goes over two stiles and after a ladder-stile, zigzags down to join a track. Keep ahead to a fence-gap for a glorious view over the estuary to Barmouth **D**.

Retrace your steps up to the footpath post at the T-junction **C**, here rejoining the shorter walk, and keep ahead along the track, parallel to the wall on the left. Turn left through a gap in that wall along a walled track, turn right at a public footpath sign through another wall-gap and head across to a ladder-stile. Climb it, follow a fairly straight and well-waymarked path across crags, go through a wall-gap, keep ahead, later by a wall on the left, and turn left over another ladder-stile.

Continue to a footpath post, head downhill to go through a wall-gap, bear left to pass through another gap, turn right and descend, by a wall on the right, to a lane at a bend **E**. Keep ahead uphill along the lane, going round several sharp bends and through a metal gate, to return to the start. ●

# Ty Mawr and the Pontcysyllte Aqueduct

| | | GPS waypoints | |
|---|---|---|---|
| **Start** | Ty Mawr Country Park | 🖉 | SJ 283 414 |
| **Distance** | 6 miles (9.7km). Shorter version 3 miles (4.8km) | Ⓐ | SJ 270 420 |
| | | Ⓑ | SJ 268 421 |
| **Approximate time** | 3 hours (1½ hours for shorter version) | Ⓒ | SJ 259 423 |
| | | Ⓓ | SJ 251 419 |
| **Parking** | Ty Mawr Country Park | Ⓔ | SJ 249 417 |
| **Refreshments** | Café and pub at Trevor Canal Basin | Ⓕ | SJ 268 421 |
| **Ordnance Survey maps** | Landranger 117 (Chester & Wrexham), Explorer 256 (Wrexham) | | |

*There is pleasant waterside walking to be had on this route, beside the River Dee as well as along the towpath of the Llangollen branch of the Shropshire Union Canal, but the most impressive feature of the route is the towering and dramatic Pontcysyllte Aqueduct which carries the canal over the Dee Valley. The walk climbs up beside the aqueduct but the shorter version omits most of the canalside walking.*

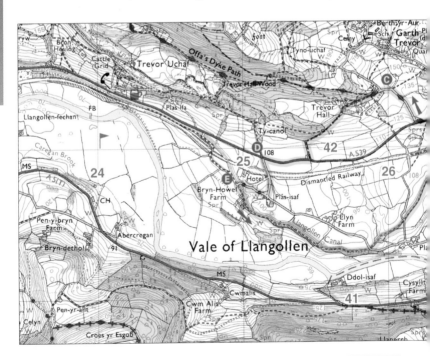

 Ty Mawr Country Park has excellent facilities for families, including tame animals and a variety of farm stock, and is an ideal place to start this largely level walk in the valley of the river Dee. Put your back to the Visitor Centre entrance and turn left, walk along the right-edge of the tarred play area and climb a stile beside a gate at the far end. Turn right and go through a gap in a fence – there's a fingerpost here 'Country Park Walk and Aqueduct.' The surfaced path gradually descends and bends left, passing by donkey, goat and sheep enclosures.

Soon after the path levels out, turn right through a gate signed 'Footpath to Aqueduct'. Drop down the steps and follow the boardwalk through a copse to reach riverside meadows. The surfaced path skirts these above the Dee, with views ahead (when the trees are not in leaf) to the aqueduct. Beyond the wide concrete bridge, pass to the right of the pumping station and trace the path through to a point beneath Pontcysyllte Aqueduct. This was designed by the renowned canal engineers Thomas Telford and William Jessop and opened in 1805, carrying the Llangollen branch of the Shropshire Union Canal at a height of 127ft (38m) above the River Dee. At over 1000ft (305m) in length it is one of the true engineering marvels of the Industrial Revolution, a giant technological leap for the time.

**A** Look for the steps on the right immediately before the aqueduct and ascend these, pass under the last arch and walk up to a road. Turn right, cross a bridge over the canal by Trevor Basin and turn left on to the towpath, here joining Offa's Dyke Path. Turn left over the first footbridge and continue along the other bank of the canal.

*At an Offa's Dyke Path fingerpost* **F***, turn left for the shorter walk, picking up route directions from the next point at which* **F** *appears in the text.*

For the full walk turn right over the next footbridge **B**, bear left and head

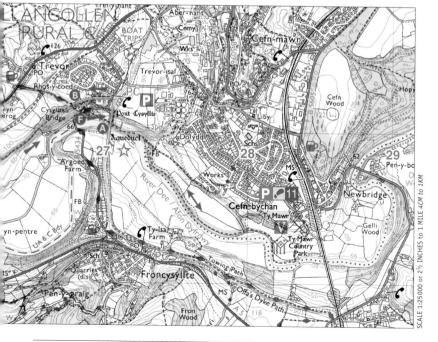

SCALE 1:25000 or 2½ INCHES to 1 MILE 4CM to 1KM

*Boat on Pontcysyllte Aqueduct*

diagonally across a field to a stile. Climb it, turn left to walk below the embankment of a disused railway and the path bends right to pass through a tunnel. Turn right, follow the path to the left and continue along an enclosed tarmac path, climbing steps to a road. Turn left, cross the road and walk the pavement to reach, on your right, Trevor Hall Road. Turn along this and trace the quiet lane to a right-hand bend. **C** Here, fork left along the gravelled drive, signed as Offa's Dyke Path. Keep ahead on this as Offa's Dyke Path departs to the right; in the trees to your left is the little 18th century estate church.

Just before reaching Trevor Hall, turn left and climb a stile next to a field gate, then bear right down the descending track beside a fence on your left. Pass below the woods and bend left to a stile, then a second one near a house and walk ahead to the road. Turn right on the narrow pavement.

**D** In 300 yds (274m) turn left along the lane signed for Bryn Howel Hotel. Walk past the hotel driveway and on to a junction. Turn right along the roughening lane (there's a 'Low Bridge' restriction sign here) and walk to and across the canal bridge.

**E** Circle back-right underneath this bridge, putting the canal on your left and joining the tranquil, tree-lined towpath. There are pleasant views of the River Dee below and the surrounding hills, and later Pontcysyllte Aqueduct comes into sight again. At a metal bridge (No 33) you briefly rejoin the outward route but at an Offa's Dyke Path fingerpost **F**, bear right off the towpath and drop down the path to a driveway. Look half-right for a waymarked flight of steps leading down to a road. For a great view of the aqueduct and River Dee divert right down to a bridge (c.200 yds/183m); otherwise turn left uphill and walk to the left-hand bend where a fingerpost directs you right, back onto the outward leg of the walk and the steps down beside the aqueduct. Simply retrace the route back to Ty Mawr Country Park, with the graceful railway viaduct as a background. ●

# Chirk and the River Ceiriog

| | | GPS waypoints |
|---|---|---|
| **Start** | Chirk | |
| **Distance** | 6 miles (9.7km) | ✎ SJ 291 376 |
| **Approximate time** | 3 hours | Ⓐ SJ 283 377 |
| **Parking** | Chirk | Ⓑ SJ 281 378 |
| **Refreshments** | Pubs and café at Chirk, pub by Chirk Bridge | Ⓒ SJ 263 389 |
| | | Ⓓ SJ 264 374 |
| | | Ⓔ SJ 267 370 |
| **Ordnance Survey maps** | Landranger 126 (Shrewsbury & Oswestry), Explorers 240 (Oswestry) and 256 (Wrexham) | Ⓕ SJ 280 371 |
| | | Ⓖ SJ 290 372 |

*After an attractive walk across the parkland surrounding Chirk Castle, with fine views of the great border fortress, the route joins Offa's Dyke Path and drops into the lovely Ceiriog Valley. It then climbs and continues along the south side of the valley before descending again to the river. The final stretch keeps by the Ceiriog, crossing delightful meadows and passing under the adjacent 19th-century viaduct and 18th-century aqueduct, built to carry different modes of transport across the valley and both engineering triumphs of their respective eras.*

Note that this route can only be walked between 1 April and 30 September as part of it, between Ⓑ and Ⓒ, uses a National Trust permissive path which is only open between those dates.

✎ Start at the crossroads in the village centre by the medieval church and turn along Church Street. Take the first turning on the left, by the war memorial, keep ahead over first a railway bridge and then a canal bridge, and at a public footpath sign turn right Ⓐ through a gap-stile. Follow the path ahead through the woods, keeping to the left-hand path and looking for a wooden handgate down to the left in 200 yds (182m). Use this and walk up the sloping field to another handgate into a lane.

Ⓑ Cross into the entry virtually opposite and take a handgate beside a field gate. *This is the start of the permissive path through Chirk Park,*

*open only between 1 April and 30 September. It is well marked by large, white-tipped posts.* Keep to the left edge of the field to use another handgate beside a field gate, from which head half-right across the parkland to use a handgate through a fence. Turn left, shortly use another handgate *(not the one on your left)* and soon join the line of the inner-estate wall on your left. Drift right to find a stile onto the main castle drive at a T-junction. Go ahead along the road towards the car park.

On this part of the walk there are impressive views of Chirk Castle, completed in 1310 but regularly altered and modernised over the centuries. Unlike most of the other border fortresses, it has been continuously occupied since it was built, mostly by the Myddleton family. It is now a National Trust property and its elegant state rooms and formal gardens are well worth a visit. Keep right at the fork into the car park. Stay alongside the left edge of the car park to the very end at a cattle-grid, here taking the first of a series of handgates beside field gates, all marked by white-tipped posts. Simply remain along the left edge of the pastures to reach a tarred lane at a bend.

**C** Immediately past the lodge house on your left, turn left over the stile, joining Offa's Dyke Path (marked by an acorn logo). Trace the field road to and past a redundant stile and ahead to a ridge-top stile. Continue ahead along the right edge of the woodland to another stile beside a metal gate. Beyond this the path steepens, dropping to a stile into a rough lane. All the while there are fine views down into the Ceiriog Valley. Turn left down this lane, which becomes tarred at a farm. Remain on it to reach a junction above some cottages. Here turn left and trace the lane all the way to the main road. Take the lane opposite (entering Shropshire here), cross the bridge over the River Ceiriog and rise steeply to a T-junction.

**D** Turn left and remain on the lane for about ½ mile (800m) to a left-bend immediately past an old school. **E** Turn left here down the old lane marked by multiple waymark discs. This gives out between a cottage and a barn; keep ahead here through two close-spaced gates and along the grassy path to a

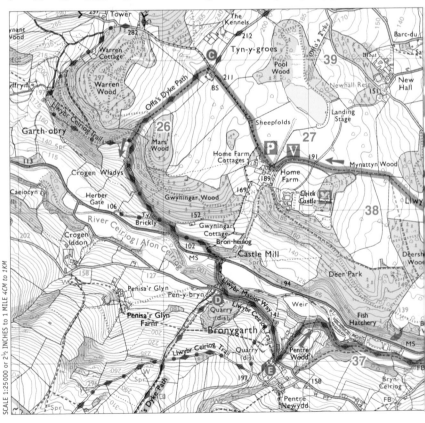

*The viaduct and aqueduct at Chirk*

stile. Climb it and bear right to reach a stile into the Woodland Trust's Pentre Wood. Climb this and join the path; in 150 yds (137m) climb the flight of steps on your right, then remain on the path as it soon drops back down more steps and comes close to the River Ceiriog,

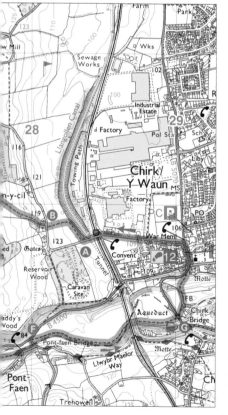

eventually to leave the woods and enter a meadow. Stick with the path close to the riverside trees; this eventually becomes a wider track and rises to a stile beside a gate at the foot of a rake of cottages. Turn left to a T-junction and left again to cross Pont-faen bridge.

**F** Turn right into the field immediately beyond the bridge and pick up the path that roughly follows the riverbank. Ahead, two multi-arched structures march across the valley. The nearest is a 19th century railway viaduct; the farthest is Thomas Telford's aqueduct carrying the Llangollen branch of the Shropshire Union Canal across the valley, impressive but not as amazing as his Pontcysyllte Aqueduct across the River Dee just a couple of miles away (see Walk 11). Use the hand-gates beneath the structures and walk ahead, shortly bending left up a fenced track to find a gate onto the road near Chirk Bridge **G**. Cross over, bear slightly left through a metal gate, at a public footpath sign, and walk along a track. Where it curves to the right, keep ahead along an enclosed path, climb a stile, turn right over a ditch and then turn left alongside it. Bear right to head uphill along a grassy path, climb a stile, and turn right along a road to return to the start. ●

# *Prestatyn Hillside*

| | | GPS waypoints |
|---|---|---|
| **Start** | Prestatyn Hillside Viewpoint car park, ½ mile (800m) north of Gwaenysgor | ✍ SJ 074 819 |
| | | Ⓐ SJ 075 810 |
| | | Ⓑ SJ 072 805 |
| **Distance** | 5½ miles (8.75km) | Ⓒ SJ 062 800 |
| **Approximate time** | 3 hours | Ⓓ SJ 062 794 |
| **Parking** | Prestatyn Hillside Viewpoint | Ⓔ SJ 065 809 |
| **Refreshments** | Pub at Gwaenysgor | Ⓕ SJ 070 813 |
| **Ordnance Survey maps** | Landranger 116 (Denbigh & Colwyn Bay), Explorers 264 (Vale of Clwyd) and 265 (Clwydian Range) | |

*On this walk in the most northerly part of the Clwydian Hills, there are extensive views over Prestatyn (which lies immediately below), Rhyl, the Vale of Clwyd and the North Wales coast. Most of the second half of the route uses first a disused railway track, and later the last stretch of Offa's Dyke Path as it climbs above Bishopswood which clothes the steep hillside.*

From the car park there are fine and extensive views over Prestatyn and Rhyl and along the coast towards the Great Orme.

✍ Start by turning right out of the car park and walking along the lane into the quiet village of Gwaenysgor. Just past the village green turn right Ⓐ along a lane, passing to the left of the small church, and a few yards after the lane becomes a rough track, take the finger-posted stone stile on the left immediately after the driveway for 'Tir Gwelyog', entering a wide grassy track.

Climb a wooden stile and then, at the bend, take the gate-side stone stile in the corner and turn right along the field edge to find another stile in a corner. Climb this and look half-left to sight a cottage. Aim for this, duck under a wire fence and head for the field corner near the cottage, where a stile gives access to a lane.

Ⓑ Turn right and remain on this lane

for ¾ mile (1.2km). Good views open out across the Vale of Clwyd and the prominent hill of Graig Fawr on your right. Keep left at a junction, remaining on the lane to reach another junction just before a National Trust car park. Ⓒ Here turn left along another lane and after ¼ mile (400m), turn right over a stile. Walk across a field, climb a stile and keep along the top edge of a sloping field, heading gently downhill. At the bottom turn left along a rough track and shortly fork right along a wider track. In 50 yds (45m) look on your right for a stile, take this and walk through a belt of trees to the edge of a meadow. Bear half-right to find a kissing-gate in the corner. Use this and turn left with the fingerpost for the Prestatyn–Dyserth Way, descending a flight of wooden steps to gain the tarred trackbed of a former railway.

Ⓓ Turn right along this and go under the bridge. This was the old London and

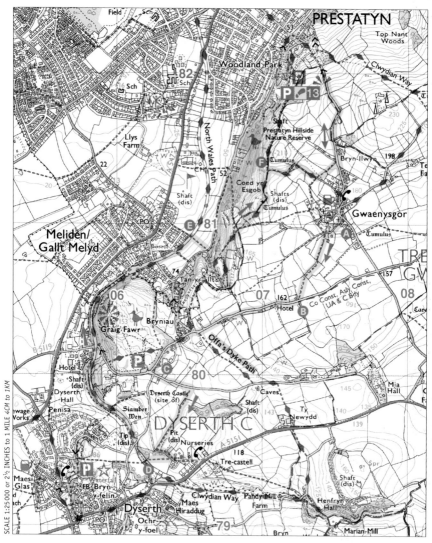

North Western Railway branch line from Prestatyn to Dyserth, and you remain on it for the next 1¼ miles (2km). Pass by the former goods shed at Meliden Station and stay on the track to reach the end of housing on your left (there's also a golf tee here). Ⓔ Turn right, use the kissing-gate and rise up the steep pasture to another kissing-gate; beyond this walk up the steep tarred lane. This becomes a wooded track, passes through a kissing-gate and in a further 100 yds (91m) meets a junction with Offa's Dyke Path (ODP). Turn left; in a further 100 yds (91m) turn left again

with the fingerpost for Prestatyn Hillside and ODP, climbing gently through Bishopswood (Coed yr Esgob), once owned by the bishops of St Asaph.

The path becomes fenced above an old quarry then rises to a three-way fingerpost, here bear right on ODP, pass through a wall gap and then rise increasingly steeply through gorse and scrub. The path levels, offering superb views off to your right to the distant horizon of Snowdonia's peaks, and then descends to pass right of a fenced mine-shaft before rising again through a thicket. Emerging from this, you'll soon reach an old fingerpost and a stile on your right. **F** Climb the stile (marked as Gwaenysgor Millennium Trail) and walk ahead along the foot of the slope towards the distant village. The path enters low woodland before reaching a kissing-gate, beyond which trace the hedged path to a walled old village well on your right. On your left here, climb the few steps, use the stile and walk ahead to another one, then stick to the right-hand side of the pasture to reach a stile into a lane. Turn left to return to the car park. ●

*Graig Fawr cutting, Meliden*

# Llyn y Gader and Beddgelert Forest

| | | GPS waypoints | |
|---|---|---|---|
| **Start** | Rhyd-Ddu, National Park car park | 🖊 | SH 571 525 |
| **Distance** | 5 miles (8km) | Ⓐ | SH 566 526 |
| **Approximate time** | 2½ hours | Ⓑ | SH 557 513 |
| **Parking** | Rhyd-Ddu | Ⓒ | SH 575 509 |
| **Refreshments** | Pub at Rhyd-Ddu, ¼ mile (400m) north of starting point | Ⓓ | SH 576 514 |
| | | Ⓔ | SH 582 525 |
| **Ordnance Survey maps** | Landranger 115 (Snowdon), Explorer OL17 (Snowdon – Conwy Valley) | | |

*This walk is through terrain that lies just to the west of Snowdon, and the last part of it uses a section of the Rhyd-Ddu Path, which is one of the most popular routes to the summit of Wales' highest mountain. For much of the way the austere Llyn y Gader is in sight, and there are dramatic views of Mynydd Mawr, the Nantlle ridge and Moel Hebog to the west, and Yr Aran, the most southerly peak of the Snowdon range, to the east. The route also touches the northern fringes of the extensive Beddgelert Forest.*

🖊 From the car park cross the road and go through a metal kissing-gate at a public footpath sign. As you walk along a slabbed path there is an imposing view ahead of the precipitous cliffs of Y Garn, part of the Nantlle ridge. On reaching the Afon Gwyrfai, follow the path to the left and then turn right to cross a footbridge over the river.

Climb a ladder-stile and turn right along a path which crosses a track to the left of a whitewashed farmhouse and continues across rough grass to join another track. Walk along the track, climb a ladder-stile on to a road and immediately turn left Ⓐ through a metal gate, at a public bridleway sign, and continue along a path by a low wall and wire fence on the right. Go through a handgate and rise to a gate, ladder-

stile and handgate. Go through and climb up to the large boulder with a white arrow painted on it. Just past this keep half-left on a gently rising path *(not the one steeply ahead)*, further painted arrows on boulders confirming the way. On this part of the route are fine views right to the Nantlle ridge and ahead to the Hebogs, whilst to the left, shapely Yr Aran rises beyond Llyn y Gader. Step over a stream, walk to and through a gate, step over another stream and bear half-right to climb more steeply and pass the foot of a spectacular water chute. The path levels out to reach a ladder-stile and handgate into Beddgelert Forest. Go through and keep ahead on the path, pass through a wall gap and descend to a wide forestry road.

**B** Turn left along this, initially through woods and then alongside a fence (left) beside reedy pastures. Keep right at the bend where a path (route-post 47) leaves to your left. At the next fork keep left to reach a T-junction (post 63). Turn left and walk this forestry road past a barrier to reach the main road *(N.B. by late 2006 the Welsh Highland Railway will cross here, so follow any appropriate directions.)*

**C** Turn left and after nearly ½ mile (800m), turn right **D** through a metal gate at a public footpath sign to Snowdon. Walk along a tarmac drive which bends left up to Ffridd Uchaf

*The imposing profile of Y Garn*

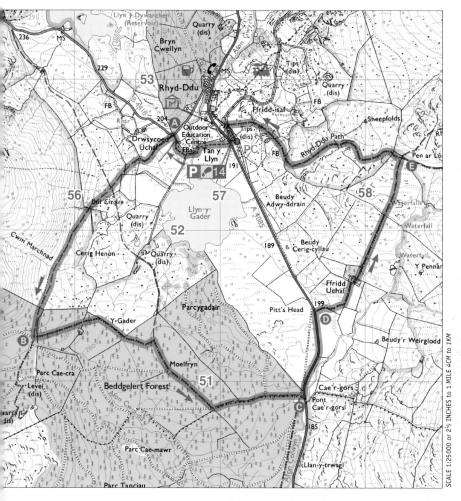

SCALE 1:25000 or 2½ INCHES to 1 MILE 4CM to 1KM

Farm, go through a metal gate, turn right between farm buildings and bear left to a handgate beside a yard gate. Use the handgate and walk up beside the conifer plantation on your left, go through a metal gate and continue uphill. To the right are grand views of Snowdon, and to the left Llyn y Gader, Y Garn and the Nantlle ridge come into view again.

Climb a ladder-stile, keep ahead across grassy moorland – although the path is only faint there are regular marker-stones – and pass to the right of an outcrop of rocks to reach a

T-junction in front of a metal gate Ⓔ. Turn left along the old quarry road here, shortly passing by (but not using) a kissing-gate on your right signed 'Footpath to Snowdon'. You're now following the Rhyd-Ddu Path; descend between rocks to a ladder-stile. Climb it and as you continue steadily downhill along a winding path, glorious views open up looking along the length of Llyn Cwellyn towards Caernarfon and the Menai Strait.

Climb two more ladder-stiles, keep ahead between old quarry workings, pass beside a metal barrier and continue to a metal kissing-gate. Go through and turn left along a track back to the start. ●

# *Elwy Valley*

| | | | |
|---|---|---|---|
| **Start** | Llanfair Talhaiarn | **GPS waypoints** | |
| **Distance** | 5 miles (8km) | 🖉 SH 927 702 | |
| **Approximate time** | 2½ hours | Ⓐ SH 933 709 | |
| | | Ⓑ SH 951 712 | |
| **Parking** | Llanfair Talhaiarn | Ⓒ SH 949 706 | |
| **Refreshments** | Pubs at Llanfair Talhaiarn | Ⓓ SH 940 707 | |
| | | Ⓔ SH 935 704 | |
| **Ordnance Survey maps** | Landranger 116 (Denbigh & Colwyn Bay), Explorer 264 (Vale of Clwyd) | | |

*Starting from the picturesque old mining village of Llanfair Talhaiarn, this walk takes in a peaceful and remote section of the beautiful valley of the Afon Elwy, an area beloved of the renowned Victorian poet Gerard Manley Hopkins. Fringing the tributary Aled Valley, it then rises to the modest summit of Mynydd Bodran – at just 942ft (287m) the views on a clear day are extraordinary, with most of Snowdonia's highest peaks forming the western horizon, the Clwydian range to the east and the rolling Denbighshire Moors to the south.* This route takes advantage of the new 'Open Access' legislation on Bodran; it also encounters huge areas of (in summer) high bracken, so choose a dry period or expect a good soaking.

🖉 The walk begins by the old bridge over the River Elwy on the edge of the pleasant village of Llanfair Talhaiarn. Turn left over the bridge and immediately turn right onto a tarred riverside path, heading downstream. Ascend steps to climb a stile, cross a road, descend steps to climb another stile and continue along the right edge of meadows beside the river, climbing a stile and following the curve of the river to the left. Climb another stile and turn right to cross a footbridge over the Elwy. Turn left, climb a stile and ascend a steep and potentially slippery path through trees – a wire fence and handrail on the left is helpful – bending right to emerge on to a lane Ⓐ. Turn left along the lane, which curves right, and where

it ends by a cottage keep ahead uphill along an enclosed path to a metal gate.

Go through and continue along an undulating path – narrow and engulfed by bracken at times, but discernible – that contours along the side of Mynydd Bodran, passing through a series of gates. The views from here over the hilly and well-wooded Elwy and Aled valleys are most attractive. On meeting a track bear right along it, going through three metal gates, to reach a T-junction. Ⓑ Turn right, keep right at a fork and go through an electric gate. The instructions are faded – essentially press the button to open the gate; an electronic eye should close it, if not then press again to close it. Walk into the yard and pass right of the farmhouse to

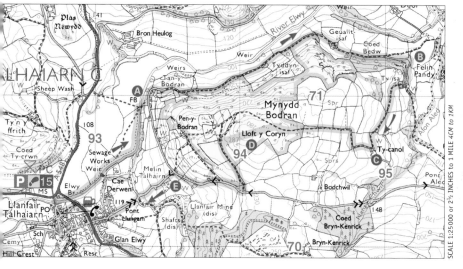

use a metal gate. Bear half-right up the slope, soon turning left along an old field road to reach a metal gate below a line of oaks. Trace the sunken track beyond to and through another gate, then look for a stile virtually in-line with the distant farmhouse. Climb this and then the next stile just up field.

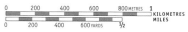

**C** Turn right and head uphill along the field edge; at the top corner use the metal gate and turn right to pass through another one. Stick with the right-hand edge of this sloping pasture, ignore the gates in the first corner and

*Looking over the Elwy Valley*

turn left to rise along the right-hand field edge to reach and climb a stile just in from the corner.

This marks the edge of Open Access country, and also the fringe of a veritable forest of bracken in the summer months. There are many indistinct sheep-tracks; the most forgiving route is to head slightly right, using several rocky outcrops as guidance and gradually gaining height up these easy slopes of Mynydd Bodran. The bracken eventually gives way to a landscape of low-growing,

rounded gorse bushes – now simply plot a course to the summit of this hilltop, pausing here to enjoy the sublime 360-degree view across North Wales.

**D** Look west (towards the Snowdonia horizon); at the slope foot is a white-painted bungalow. Make your way down through gorse and heather to gain the access road just to the left of this. Turn left along this track and follow it through a gate to reach a tarred road; turn right down this and walk downhill to a junction. **E** Keep left and remain on this lane past minor junctions to reach a crossroads with the main A544 road at the edge of Llanfair Talhaiarn. Carefully cross and turn right, downhill, to find a fingerpost and low wooden bollards on your left immediately before a bridge over the Afon Elwy. Take this tarred path, keep left through a handgate at a split and walk between buildings to emerge beside The Swan pub in the village square. Turn right to return to the car park. ●

*Llanfair Talhaiarn*

# Llyn Padarn

| | | GPS waypoints | |
|---|---|---|---|
| **Start** | Llanberis, village car park beside Llyn Padarn | | |
| | | SH 577 604 | |
| **Distance** | 5½ miles (8.9km) | Ⓐ SH 575 607 | |
| | | Ⓑ SH 559 623 | |
| **Approximate time** | 3 hours | Ⓒ SH 575 617 | |
| **Parking** | Village car park at Llanberis | Ⓓ SH 586 604 | |
| **Refreshments** | Pubs and cafés at Llanberis | Ⓔ SH 585 601 | |
| **Ordnance Survey maps** | Landranger 115 (Snowdon), Explorers OL17 (Snowdon – Conwy Valley) and 263 (Anglesey East) | | |

*Llyn Padarn is situated at the foot of Snowdon and this straightforward circuit of the lake, which uses a combination of a disused railway track, lane, woodland and lakeside paths and old quarry tracks, provides a series of memorable views of the surrounding mountains, including spectacular ones of Snowdon itself, for relatively little effort. As well as pleasant walking beside the lake, there is attractive woodland on the slopes above its eastern side, interesting remains of the slate-quarrying industry that once dominated this part of Snowdonia, and a brief detour to the ruins of Dolbadarn Castle which occupy a commanding position between Llyn Padarn and the adjacent Llyn Peris.*

Its splendid situation below Snowdon and between two lakes has enabled the former slate-quarrying village of Llanberis to become a major tourist resort and walking centre. It is the starting point for ascents of Snowdon, both on foot and by the Snowdon Mountain Railway. There is another railway that runs along the shore of Llyn Padarn, and the many physical remains of the once great slate-quarrying industry only add to its appeal and interest.

Start by walking down to the lake and turn left on to a path which curves left to the road. Turn right and take the first turning on the right Ⓐ to continue along a broad tarmac drive, the bed of a former railway. After

passing through a barrier, the drive becomes a rough, tree-lined track (Lon Las Peris) which keeps beside Llyn Padarn. Walk through the short tunnel and keep ahead on the fenced path to reach the main road. Cross this, turn right along the verge and climb the ladder-stile about 70 yds (64m) away on the left. This puts you on the line of the abandoned A4086 road. Pass by a superfluous ladder-stile and remain on the old tarred road, climb a second stile and continue to a nearby road junction beside a cottage. Fork right here to cross an old bridge at the foot of Llyn Padarn. From here there is a magnificent view looking down the length of the lake towards the Llanberis Pass, with the

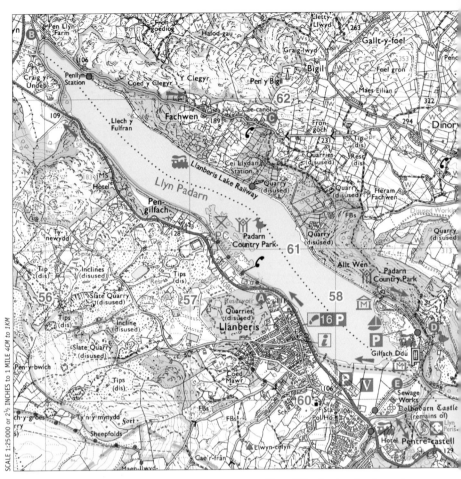

SCALE 1:25000 or 2½ INCHES to 1 MILE 4CM to 1KM

summit of Snowdon clearly visible.

Turn right **B** along a narrow lane, signposted to Fachwen, which climbs steadily through woodland above the lake and after one mile (1.6km) – just after passing a telephone box – turn right **C** at a public footpath sign, through a metal gate on to a path that descends through trees. This soon joins a tarred lane; walk down this, which gradually winds down through lovely woodland, passing remote cottages and roughening as it passes beneath an old quarry bridge. Narrowing, it eventually reaches a footbridge across a tumbling stream.

Cross it, turn right, then turn left through a kissing-gate and head

steadily uphill, via steps in places, to a superb viewpoint overlooking the lake. Now the path descends again, at a fork take the right-hand, lower, slabbed path, pass through a wall-gap and continue across a terrace in front of the Quarry Hospital, now a visitor centre but once the hospital for the employees of the Dinorwic Quarry Company. Head downhill along a tarmac track, go under an arch and pass below the former workings of Vivian Quarry with a pool below. The quarry was named after W.W. Vivian, who was manager of the Dinorwic Quarry Company at the end of the 19th century.

Just before the lane curves right to pass under a bridge, take the walled path on the right and walk a few paces to cross the steep rail-tracks of an old quarry incline. Turn down beside these, descending to the car park here at the heart of the Welsh Slate Museum complex. There are myriad attractions here. The main body of the museum is housed in the former workshops of the Dinorwic Quarry Company and contains much of the original machinery, including a large water-wheel. At their height in the Victorian era, when demand for Welsh slate was at its greatest, the Dinorwic quarries were the largest anywhere in the world and employed over 3000 men. The Llanberis Lake Railway, the terminus of which is next to the museum, was constructed to carry the slate to the docks at Port Dinorwic on the Menai Strait. The quarries closed down in 1969.

🄳 To continue the walk from the complex, join the access road with the fenced railway on your left and the main museum buildings to your right. Walk along this and through a wrought-iron gate to a T-junction with another road. Here turn right, immediately crossing a bridge across the spillway (note the retractable barriers) linking the twin lakes Llyn Peris and Llyn Padarn. Off to your left here is the entrance to 'Electric

*Looking towards Snowdon from Llyn Padarn*

Mountain', a vast underground hydro-electric power station created in the bowels of the former Dinorwig Slate Quarries; it's also a very popular visitor attraction. In a further 300 yds (274m) turn left down steps, cross a footbridge over a stream, go through a metal gate and follow a path up steps to Dolbadarn Castle, whose circular keep, situated on a rocky knoll above the lake, still guards the southern end of the Llanberis Pass. It is a native Welsh castle, built by Llewellyn the Great in the early 13th century.

Retrace your steps back down to the road and cross into the car park opposite. At the far-left corner a kissing-gate leads onto a surfaced path. Turn right along this and wind with it around to pass beneath a bridge carrying the Llanberis Lake Railway. 🄴 In a few paces go straight over the wider path (do not cross the footbridge on your right) to join a grassy path that passes to the left of a slate hut and then strikes across rough meadows here at the head of Llyn Padarn. A few old kissing-gates and flat bridges lead to a footbridge beside an adventure playground, beyond which follow the well-used path beside the lake and through to the village car park. ●

# Lledr Valley

| | | GPS waypoints | |
|---|---|---|---|
| **Start** | Dolwyddelan | ✏ | SH 737 521 |
| **Distance** | 6½ miles (10.5km) | Ⓐ | SH 739 520 |
| **Approximate time** | 3 hours | Ⓑ | SH 773 537 |
| **Parking** | Dolwyddelan, car park and picnic area by station | Ⓒ | SH 770 538 |
| **Refreshments** | Pubs and cafés at Dolwyddelan | Ⓓ | SH 756 537 |
| **Ordnance Survey maps** | Landranger 115 (Snowdon), Explorer OL18 (Harlech, Porthmadog & Bala) | | |

*This is a walk that provides a succession of outstanding views over the surrounding mountains, especially of Moel Siabod and Snowdon, plus attractive woodland and riverside walking, for only a modest effort. The first half is along a broad and undulating track, much of it through woodland, and the return is along tree-lined paths and lanes and across lush meadows bordering the lovely River Lledr.*

The village of Dolwyddelan is situated below the spectacular rugged slopes of Moel Siabod in the Lledr Valley. It has a small, largely unrestored 16th-century church, and about ¾ mile (1.2km) to the west is Dolwyddelan Castle, reputed

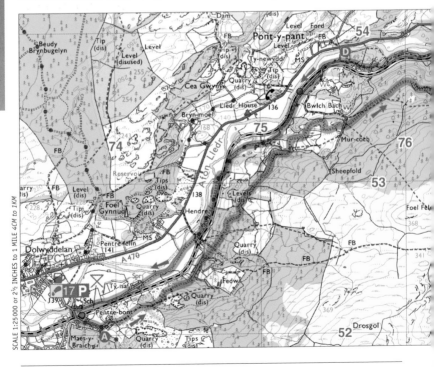

birthplace of Llewellyn the Great. The castle is in sight for much of this route and was one of the principal residences of the princes of Gwynedd. During the English conquest it was occupied by Llewellyn ap Gruffydd, last native prince of Wales, before being captured by Edward I in 1282. At the end of the Middle Ages it fell into disuse and ruin; the main surviving parts are the fine 12th-century keep, which was partially rebuilt in the 19th century, and the 13th-century west tower.

🔖 Start by turning left out of the car park and picnic area, turn left again to cross the railway bridge and at a T-junction bear left along a lane. Walk uphill and where the lane ends by the last house, turn left on to a track, **Ⓐ** passing in front of houses.

Keep along this clear, broad, winding and gently undulating track for the next 2½ miles (4km), negotiating

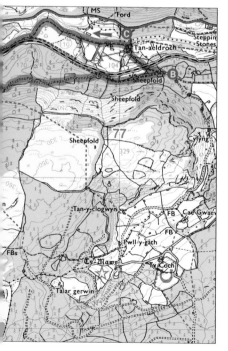

several gates and stiles. At the start there are some abandoned slate-quarries and for much of the way the track passes through attractive woodland. The more open stretches provide some superb views to the left across the Lledr Valley, with Snowdon and Moel Siabod prominent on the skyline, plus the impressively sited Dolwyddelan Castle. The place at which to leave this forestry road is difficult to spot and is not waymarked. Shortly after coming close to and above the railway, you'll reach a series of small, walled fields visible close-by down to your left. About 150 yds (137m) past the end of the last one, a very narrow path angles sharply back to your left (there's also one forking off acutely to the right, and at this point you're below a very lofty, wooded crag on your right).

**Ⓑ** Turn sharp left here; the path parallels the forestry road for a short distance, then widens into a woodland path and falls to pass under a railway bridge. Bear left and remain on the path, dropping to a ladder-stile to the right of the farmhouse grounds. Climb this and go ahead a few paces before forking left at a fingerpost 'River Walk to Dolwyddelan' beside the gateway to the farm.

**Ⓒ** A narrow, overgrown path drops down to become a stony, slabbed riverside way. Remain on this to climb a ladder-stile into woods; in a further 100 yds (91m) fork right at a waymark post, taking the lower path which is uneven underfoot, so exercise care as you walk through this lovely, gorged section of the Lledr Valley. Occasional waymarked posts confirm you're on the right path; eventually you'll reach a waymarked wooden handgate through a wall. Use this, and a metal gate a short distance away, beyond which the path hugs a ledge between the river and the railway embankment before traversing wood pasture.

**D** An outdoor centre soon appears in trees off to your right. At the reedy field-end, go through the old metal gate and walk up to a driveway. Cross straight over to walk a rising path that climbs to join a tarred drive to the left of a hotel. Bear left and at the nearby bend fork left along a tarred lane which leads to and past Pont-y-pant Station to where it ends at a farm. Keep ahead through a metal gate and walk along an undulating track, later keeping beside the railway line on the right. Go through a metal gate, turn right through another to pass under a railway bridge and turn left along a path across lovely riverside meadows. Now come more splendid views of the river, Moel Siabod and Snowdon.

Pass to the right of farm buildings, go through a gate and keep ahead along a track, passing by an attractive old clapper-bridge over the Lledr on the right. The tarmac track continues across meadows, keeps to the left of another farm – there are some gates to negotiate here – and leads directly back to the starting point. ●

_The Lledr Valley_

# Vale of Ffestiniog

| | | GPS waypoints |
|---|---|---|
| Start | Rhŷd-y-sarn parking and picnic area, beside A496, ½ mile (800m) north of its junction with B4391 – look for the telephone box by a lay-by near cottages | ✏ SH 690 422 |
| | | Ⓐ SH 680 423 |
| | | Ⓑ SH 665 411 |
| | | Ⓒ SH 664 408 |
| Distance | 5½ miles (8.9km) | Ⓓ SH 667 412 |
| Approximate time | 3 hours | Ⓔ SH 687 416 |
| Parking | Rhŷd-y-sarn | Ⓕ SH 692 419 |
| Refreshments | Pubs at Maentwrog | |
| Ordnance Survey maps | Landranger 124 (Porthmadog & Dolgellau), Explorer OL18 (Harlech, Porthmadog & Bala) | |

*The first part of the walk is through the delightful, dense, steep-sided woodlands that clothe the northern slopes of the Vale of Ffestiniog, part of the Coedydd Maentwrog National Nature Reserve. There is a succession of superb views down the vale and on several occasions the path crosses the track of the steam-hauled Ffestiniog Railway. After descending into the valley and making a brief detour into Maentwrog, the route continues by the Afon Dwyryd before a final wooded stretch. Although this is not a lengthy or strenuous walk, there is quite a lot of climbing, especially on the first stage.*

✏ Facing the picnic site – on the opposite side of the road from the parking area – turn right, almost immediately turn left along a track, at a public footpath sign, and go through a metal gate. The track curves to the left – where it ends, keep ahead along a path to go through a metal gate. Keep ahead on the woodland path, bending left to a gate leading into the Coed Cymerau National Nature Reserve. This is an area of oak woodland, probably a remnant of the vast woodlands that used to cover much of North Wales.

Head uphill beside the lovely surging river – there are lots of small waterfalls – turn left over a footbridge and continue climbing quite steeply. The woodland becomes a conifer plantation. Walking by a second Nature Reserve board, stay on the main path, stepping over a brook and shortly passing through a broken wall. At the top of the woods climb the ladder-stile and walk ahead beside a wall and through high bracken. Climb a further ladder-stile and turn left; shortly bear right up along a rough lane and follow this along the woodland edge, keeping left at a fork.

Ⓐ The old lane levels out at a point where the trackbed of the old route of the Ffestiniog Railway is reached – there's a ruined overbridge 150 yds (137m) ahead. Turn sharp-left to walk along the trackbed, still marked by old wooden sleepers. Go through a gate into Dduallt Station and walk ahead (crossing the nearest railway line) to

*The Afon Goedol*

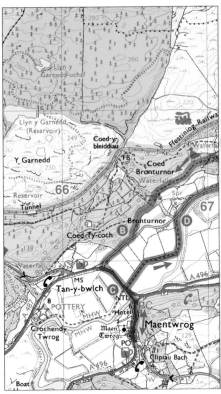

pass to the right of the station building. Just beyond the abandoned house on the right, re-cross the line, climb the ladder-stile and turn left along a path parallel to the railway. Go under the railway bridge and follow the path through bracken and via two wall gaps to another ladder-stile. On this part of the walk the views down the wooded Vale of Ffestiniog and over the surrounding mountains are superb and, at times, the buildings of Trawsfynydd Nuclear Power Station appear on the horizon.

Climb the stile, cross the line again, climb another ladder-stile and turn right on to a path that descends along the side of the valley to join a track in front of a house. Keep ahead along the steadily descending track – it later becomes a tarmac track – and where it does a U-bend to the left, keep ahead over a stile at a public footpath sign. Head down to cross a stream below a waterfall, continue downhill to a kissing-gate, go through, bear left and descend steeply to a concrete track. Turn right uphill, passing to the left of a house, and cross a footbridge over a stream. Bear half-left off the bridge on a level path through to a handgate. Go through this and trace the undulating path through superb woodlands, gradually dropping to reach a tarred lane. **B** Turn right to the main road and turn left along it. Just before the bridge across the Afon Dwyryd the route turns left, through a kissing-gate and onto an embankment **C**. For a brief detour into Maentwrog, instead keep ahead and fork right, cross the river and at a T-junction turn right through the village, built in the early 19th century by William Oakley, a local slate magnate. The spire of the Victorian church is appropriately covered in slate.

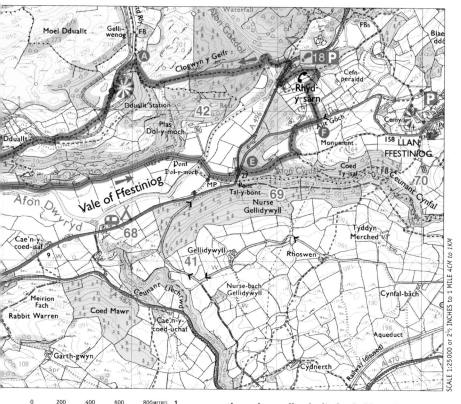

Retrace your steps over the bridge, turn right through a metal kissing-gate **C** at a public footpath sign, and walk along the top of an embankment. Along this stretch of the route you can enjoy the fine views looking up the wooded vale, framed by mountains and with lush riverside meadows on either side. On approaching the river the path curves left to a gate. Go through, turn right **D** and keep along a quiet, attractive lane for the next 1½ miles (2.4km) – initially beside the river, then bending right to cross it, and finally continuing by a tributary stream (Afon Cynfal) up to a road.

Turn sharp right to a junction, turn sharp left, in the Ffestiniog direction, and at a public footpath sign, turn right over a stone stile **E**. Head uphill through woodland, climb a ladder-stile, keep ahead to emerge from the trees and walk alongside a wall. At the tumbled corner, step through the gap and turn left, wall now on your left, and walk through to a stile onto a road. Turn right and walk uphill for 200 yds (183m); turn left at a public footpath sign **F** go through a gate and walk down the enclosed path. After going through a metal gate, the path heads more steeply down to go through a metal kissing-gate at the bottom.

Cross a boggy patch and bear right to walk along the bottom edge of the field to the corner, where you head up, following the right-hand edge of the field past a waymarker. Go through a gap at the top and keep straight ahead, with a wall on your left, to a stile. Cross this and bear left onto a track. Follow this downhill to a road and turn sharp right to return to the start.

# Llanrwst, Gwydyr Forest and Trefriw

| | | GPS waypoints |
|---|---|---|
| **Start** | Llanrwst | 🖊 SH 798 616 |
| **Distance** | 6 miles (9.7km) | 🅐 SH 798 614 |
| **Approximate time** | 3 hours | 🅑 SH 797 607 |
| **Parking** | Llanrwst | 🅒 SH 789 609 |
| **Refreshments** | Pubs and cafés at Llanrwst, pubs and cafés at Trefriw | 🅓 SH 781 616 |
| | | 🅔 SH 776 616 |
| **Ordnance Survey maps** | Landrangers 115 (Snowdon) and 116 (Denbigh & Colwyn Bay), Explorer OL17 (Snowdon – Conwy Valley) | 🅕 SH 780 631 |
| | | 🅖 SH 792 622 |

*The first and last parts of the walk are across attractive meadows bordering the River Conwy; most of the remainder is through woodland on the eastern slopes of Gwydyr Forest, from where there is a succession of fine views over the Conwy Valley. Historic interest is provided by three interesting churches, a 15th-century courthouse and a 17th-century bridge. Some climbing is involved through the forest but none of it is too steep or strenuous.*

The pleasant market town of Llanrwst lies on the eastern bank of the River Conwy, here spanned by a fine three-arched bridge, built in 1636 and possibly designed by Inigo Jones. On the west side of the bridge is Tu-hwnt-i'r-bont, a 15th-century former courthouse, now owned by the National Trust and used as a giftshop and tearoom. The imposing church, largely rebuilt in the 1880s, is noted for its carved rood screen and loft, and for the adjacent Gwydir Chapel, built in the 17th century as the mausoleum for the Gwynne family of Gwydir Castle. At one time the large stone coffin in it was thought to be that of Llewellyn the Great.

🖊 The walk starts in the market place in the town centre. Walk along the main road in the Betws-y-Coed direction, turn right to cross the old bridge over the River Conwy and immediately turn left 🅐 at a public footpath sign, along a tarmac path. Continue beside the river – a delightful stretch of riverside walking with grand views upstream – going through a metal kissing-gate and keeping ahead to a stile.

After climbing the stile, turn right along the right edge of a field up to a ladder-stile, climb this and turn right along a road. At a sign to Gwydyr Uchaf Chapel 🅑, turn sharp left up a tarmac drive and where the drive bends equally sharply to the right, keep ahead – just to the right of a bench – along a steep uphill path through trees, here entering Gwydyr Forest. The path curves left then right to reach a broad track; turn sharp right along it and at a fork immediately ahead, take the right-hand lower track. From this track there

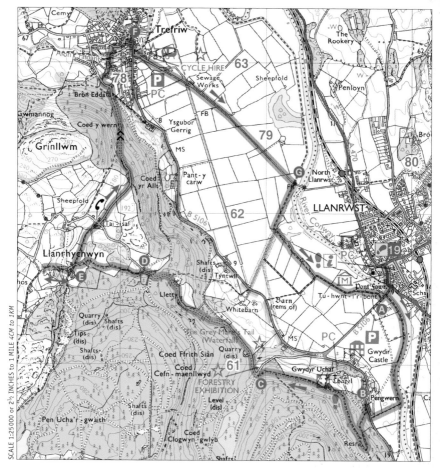

SCALE 1:25 000 or 2½ INCHES to 1 MILE 4CM to 1KM

```
0    200   400   600   800 METRES  1
                                   KILOMETRES
                                   MILES
0    200   400   600 YARDS         ½
```

are attractive views through the trees to the right, over Llanrwst and the Conwy Valley. The track passes above Gwydyr Uchaf Chapel to which a short detour can be made by turning right along a track and, where it bends right, keeping ahead down a shady path, climbing two stiles. Originally built for the Gwynne family in 1604, it has a fine painted ceiling. The home of the Gwynnes, the much-restored Tudor mansion of Gwydir Castle, is nearby.

Return to the main route, where the track continues along the edge of the forest to emerge on to a lane at a junction **C**. Take the narrow lane ahead, signposted to Llanrhychwyn,

cross a stream, and a ladder-stile on the right gives access to the Grey Mare's Tail waterfall, after decent rains a spectacular, graceful twin falls.

The lane soon starts to climb quite steeply; in ¾ mile (1.2km) you'll reach the edge of the woods. **D** On the left here, and immediately within the woods, walk along a rising, waymarked path and climb a nearby ladder-stile. Go ahead beside a fallen wall and then a wire fence, soon emerging into a small pasture. Keep along the left edge to use a stile beside a wooden gate – the way is then a wide grassy track through open oakwoods. Take another stile beside a gateway into pasture and walk ahead towards the far left corner. Just up from this is a stile into a wide, fenced track through a strand of trees.

Keep left to use a metal gate and then walk the field road to gain a rough lane just right of the farm.

Ⓔ The way is right, along the lane. *It is, however, a rewarding detour to find the remote and ancient church at Llanrhychwyn. To do so, turn left and take the track to the right of the farmhouse. Look immediately on your right for a waymarked kissing-gate onto a path up steps. Take this and climb to a second kissing-gate. Pass through a third kissing-gate near a cottage and rise to a fourth, just to the right of the little church visible in trees on the hillside.* Dedicated to St Rhychwyn, it too has connections to Llywelyn Fawr (The Great) and is a superb example of a totally unspoilt simple, early-medieval rural church, complete with slate-slabbed floor and lit by candles.

Return to the lane by the farm and walk it through to the crossroads in the tiny hamlet. Keep ahead along a narrow lane, in the Trefriw direction, and there are impressive views of the houses of Trefriw ahead, clinging to the sides of the steep hillside above the valley, as the lane descends steeply into the village. Pass by the first few houses; at the second public footpath sign on your right (just before a white-painted house,

Y Wern, on the left) turn down a short tarred ramp onto an enclosed path, dropping to a lane. Bear left down this to a junction; here go ahead along a path beside a garage and cross a footbridge over the Afon Crafnant. Walk along the winding path to a road and here turn right to a junction above an old chapel. Turn right to reach the main road in Trefriw, turn right here to reach the village centre.

Ⓕ Trefriw is noted for its woollen mill where visitors can watch the various stages in the production of tweeds and tapestries. Just to the north of the village is the Victorian spa of Trefriw Wells. Turn left opposite Trefriw Woollen Mills, passing a parking area. Continue along a straight, tarmac drive for just under one mile (1.6km) to reach a suspension bridge over the River Conwy. Do not cross it but turn right Ⓖ over a stile and walk along the top of an embankment. Pass by one stile to reach a second above gates. Climb this and turn left to climb a stile and cross a flat bridge; beyond this follow a path along the left edge of a series of fields and over a succession of stiles. Eventually climb a ladder-stile and turn left along an enclosed, hedge-lined track which bears right and continues to a road. Turn left and re-cross the old bridge over the river to return to the centre of Llanrwst. ●

*The River Conwy at Llanwrst*

# Rhaeadr Mawddach and Pistyll Cain

| | | GPS waypoints |
|---|---|---|
| **Start** | Ganllwyd, National Trust car park at south end of the village | 🥾 SH 727 243 |
| **Distance** | 7 miles (11.3km) | Ⓐ SH 727 248 |
| **Approximate time** | 3½ hours | Ⓑ SH 736 275 |
| **Parking** | Ganllwyd | Ⓒ SH 734 274 |
| **Refreshments** | None | Ⓓ SH 734 261 |
| **Ordnance Survey maps** | Landranger 124 (Porthmadog & Dolgellau), Explorer OL18 (Harlech, Porthmadog & Bala) | Ⓔ SH 729 262 |
| | | Ⓕ SH 727 263 |

*The title of this walk uses the names of the two waterfalls that are its chief focal points and most spectacular features. Almost the whole route is through the woodlands of the vast Coed-y-Brenin Forest, an easy walk mostly along broad, clear tracks with only relatively gentle climbing. From the higher and more open parts, there are fine views over the surrounding mountains of the Rhinog and Cadair Idris ranges.*

🥾 With your back to the car park, cross the road and turn right, passing the village school. Cross to the right beyond the lay-by and then fork right down the 'No Through Road' at the speed de-restriction signs. Cross the bridge over the Afon Eden Ⓐ and bear right, following this tarred lane past a telephone exchange and into magnificent fir woods. At a left bend in ½ mile (800m), fork right down a wide rough lane, passing a Geology Trail board to reach and cross a long footbridge across the Mawddach. Turn left along the forestry road beyond.

In ¼ mile (400m) fork left past a gate, the route still following the gorge of the Mawddach and confirmed by yellow-topped posts. In just over ½ mile (800m), again fork left at a junction; the roadway eventually bends sharply left, in due course emerging from the trees to unveil a view down into the gorge and the Rhaeadr Mawddach Falls.

Ⓑ Only 150 yds (137m) or so past this point, and opposite a bridleway finger-post, fork left down a steep track (marked by a white and yellow topped post) to reach and cross a stone bridge over the Afon Mawddach. Your way is left along the roadway at the far side, passing above the Rhaeadr Mawddach. In the wooded hills up to your right is the Gwynfynydd gold mine. Gold was first found here in 1863 but it was not until 1887 that it became fully exploited under William Pritchard Morgan, the Welsh gold king. The mine closed in 1916, reopened in the 1930s and is still being worked. The route continues to the left, heading downhill and bearing right to keep beside the River Gain near its confluence with the Mawddach. On the left is the site of the

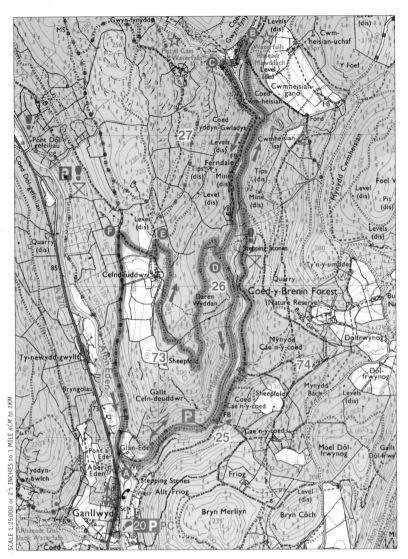

gold-mine mill. It closed a year after the mine, in 1917, was rebuilt in the 1930s but burned down in 1935 before it was completed. Sweep left across the wide, rusty metal bridge over the Afon Gain; to your right is the spectacular Pistyll Cain, after decent rain one of the most impressive falls in Snowdonia.

**C** Remain on the rough road, eventually passing the buildings at Ferndale holiday cottages. Beyond a gateway the track becomes a tarred lane, shortly reaching the Tyddyn Gwladys forestry car park. Some 160 yds (150m) beyond this look right

for a sharp turn back up along another forestry track **D**, this one marked by an orange cycle track sign and a blue Karrimor post. (*At this point you can choose to remain on the tarred lane back to Ganllwyd, or rise into the woods via Points* **E** *and* **F**.) To reach Point **E**, follow the track around a sharp left bend, continue steadily uphill, then go round a U-bend to the right and and remain on this undulating forestry road to reach, on your left in a further ½ mile

(800m), a small open area fenced in by wire fencing. At the end of this is a wooden field gate. **E** Turn back through this and walk down the track for 100 yds (91m) to reach a junction with a farm lane. Turn right here, use the gate into the horse pasture (close this gate securely if you first open it) and walk the field road through to another metal gate and a fingerpost.

**F** Turn left along the grass-centred lane above the steep-sided valley of the Afon Eden. Cadair Idris is ahead as the track – which later becomes a tarmac lane – re-enters woodland and descends, quite steeply in places, to a fork where cycle route 8 goes left. Here, remain on the tarred lane down to a cottage beside the bridge over the Afon Eden. **A** Cross the bridge, rise to the main road and walk downhill to return to the car park. ●

*The River Mawddach near Ganllwyd*

# Penmaenmawr and the Druid's Circle

| | | GPS waypoints |
|---|---|---|
| **Start** | Penmaenmawr, by the library in town centre | ✎ SH 719 762 |
| **Distance** | 4½ miles (7.2km) | Ⓐ SH 721 759 |
| **Approximate time** | 2½ hours | Ⓑ SH 721 747 |
| | | Ⓒ SH 720 746 |
| **Parking** | Penmaenmawr, car park by library | Ⓓ SH 730 759 |
| **Refreshments** | Pubs and cafés at Penmaenmawr | Ⓔ SH 727 758 |
| **Ordnance Survey maps** | Landranger 115 (Snowdon), Explorer OL17 (Snowdon – Conwy Valley) | Ⓕ SH 725 756 |

*Because the initial climb from Penmaenmawr is steep and unrelenting, it's best to take your time in order to enjoy the grand views over the mountains, the coast and the Isle of Anglesey. The route leads on to open moorland on the slopes of the Carneddau and passes the Druid's Circle, the most outstanding and atmospheric of the many prehistoric remains in this area. After a fresh and invigorating ramble across the moorland, there is a relatively easy descent back to the town.*

The small coastal town of Penmaen-mawr is squeezed between mountains and sea and hemmed in by the steep headlands on either side. Before the 19th century it was largely cut off by land, as travellers had to go over the top of the headlands – a hazardous journey – but the Victorians quarried away part of Penmaen Mawr and tunnelled a railway and road through between Conwy and Bangor. In the 19th century it became a popular seaside resort, much favoured by Gladstone, and has a fine sandy beach, but its heyday ended with changing tastes and the growth of foreign travel.

✎ Turn right out of the car park and immediately right again along Y Berllan. Take the first turning on the left – almost doubling back – then the next turning on the right and, where the road ends, keep ahead along an enclosed, hedge-lined track, the left-hand one of two beyond the road name plaque for Y Berllan. Head gently uphill to join Craiglwyd Road, turn right Ⓐ and at a public footpath sign to the Druid's Circle, turn left up a farm track.

Climb over a ladder-stile, pass to the left of the farm and at a wall corner, bear right and head up a grassy bank to go through a metal kissing-gate. Now comes the start of the steep and quite tiring climb on to the moorland above Penmaenmawr. After a few yards bear left and follow a clear, grassy, uphill path through some bracken. The benches that once offered rest stops for the thousand of visitors for whom Penmaenmawr was a popular

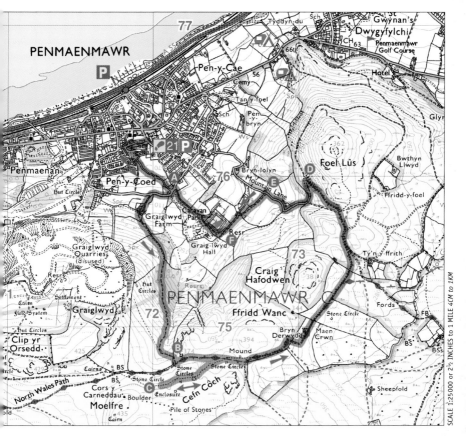

SCALE 1:25 000 or 2½ INCHES to 1 MILE 4CM to 1KM

```
0    200   400   600   800 METRES  1
|----|----|----|----|----|         | KILOMETRES
                                     MILES
0    200   400   600 YARDS  ½
```

destination are now ruinous, but the splendid bluebell woods remain, as do the superb views across the bay to the Great Orme. The path later bears to the right, becomes steeper and eventually turns left, crosses a concrete section laid over wet and boggy ground and continues up to a metal gate.

From here there is a particularly fine view of Penmaenmawr below, cradled between the steep headlands of Penmaen Mawr (from which the town gets its name) and Penmaen-bach.

Go through the gate, turn right and follow the wall to a small stone enclosure, then turn left **B** on to a track which is part of the North Wales Path. The wide, grassy track passes by a North

Wales Path waymark post and rises gradually along the moorland edge. Back to your left are the fringes of the imposing Graiglwyd granite quarries, stone from which was used to cobble the streets of Lancashire's industrial towns and cities. Much earlier, Neolithic craftsmen made stone axes here; products of this 'Graig Llwyd Axe Factory' were traded across the rest of Britain and Europe. In the background is Puffin Island, off the eastern tip of Anglesey. Upon reaching a second North Wales Path waymark post at a distinct left-hand kink in the track, divert sharply back right along a grassy path that climbs directly to the stones breaking the horizon.

**C** The stones are those of Maeni Hirion, the Druid's Circle, although they stretch farther back into the mists of

*Along the way at Foel Lus*

time than the Druids, dating back to the Bronze Age perhaps 4000 years ago. There's a smaller stone circle beyond, and the moors of these northern fringes of the Carneddau range are liberally littered with standing stones, cists and burials.

Retrace your steps to the North Wales Path and continue eastwards, soon picking up the line of a wall on your right. Follow the direction of a footpath post to the right, go through a metal gate, keep ahead and at the next footpath post, turn left along a beautiful tree-lined track, passing to the right of a house. In the field on the right is a standing stone.

Keep ahead along the track, going through a metal gate. Continue ahead, ignoring a metal gate and North Wales Path sign off to the right. Go through another metal gate, eventually bearing left to join a track which starts to descend. Turn sharp left in front of gateposts **D** to continue more steeply

downhill – the track becomes a tarmac one. Go over a cattle-grid and, ignoring a footpath sign, continue ahead as far as the next public footpath sign on the left.

**E** Climb steps on your left here opposite a covered reservoir, go through a metal kissing-gate and trace the right-hand edge of sheep pasture, passing above a large old country house. Keep ahead along a wider field-edge track bounded by a line of tall trees. Look for the low ladder-stile on your right halfway along this strand of trees, climb it and bear left alongside the fence above a trout fishery. **F** Bend right and remain on the enclosed path between the fishery and a caravan park. At the bottom take a kissing-gate beside a metal gate and turn left to descend the tarred drive. Upon reaching the T-junction with a lane, turn left and then immediately right into an enclosed path, here rejoining the outward leg of the walk at **A**. Simply retrace this initial stretch back to the start. ●

# Penycloddiau and Moel Arthur

| | | GPS waypoints |
|---|---|---|
| **Start** | Moel Famau Country Park, Llangwyfan car park, 1 mile (1.6km) east of Llangwyfan village | SJ 139 667 |
| **Distance** | 7½ miles (12.1km) | Ⓐ SJ 121 689 |
| **Approximate time** | 3½ hours | Ⓑ SJ 130 664 |
| **Parking** | Llangwyfan car park | Ⓒ SJ 140 656 |
| **Refreshments** | None | Ⓓ SJ 147 657 |
| **Ordnance Survey maps** | Landranger 116 (Denbigh & Colwyn Bay), Explorer 265 (Clwydian Range) | |

*The first and last parts of the route involve two ascents and descents as you follow Offa's Dyke Path along the ridge of the Clwydian Hills, passing the prehistoric hillforts of Penycloddiau and Moel Arthur. The remainder is along clearly defined and generally flat tracks that contour along the side of the hills, making for easy, attractive and trouble-free walking. There are some pleasant wooded stretches and continuously fine views across the broad Vale of Clwyd.*

Begin by going through a gate, at the fork in front take the right-hand track and at the next fork a few yards ahead, take the right-hand, uphill path, following Offa's Dyke Path waymarks. The path runs parallel to the track and heads uphill, steeply at times, along the right edge of conifers to a stile.

Turn right over it, here crossing the outer earth-works of Penycloddiau, an Iron Age hillfort, and continue uphill across the middle of the fort. After passing a cairn, you reach the outer defences again and at this point the views from this ridgetop track, to the right

*On the shoulder of Moel Arthur*

*A pleasant track in the Clwydian Hills*

and left and ahead along the rolling Clwydian range, are magnificent. Bear right for a few yards and then turn left to continue across heathery moorland, descending to a stile. Climb it, cross a low rise and then continue gradually downhill on the wide path, following Offa's Dyke Path waymarks to another stile just beyond a stand of pine trees.

**Ⓐ** Do not climb this one but turn left on to a broad track by a wire fence on the right. Keep along this winding track for the next 2½ miles (4km), going through several gates, passing by the edge of attractive woodland at one stage, and with glorious views across the Vale of Clwyd all the time. Finally the track bears left and keeps below conifers to reach a lane **Ⓑ**.

Bear left, follow the lane around a right-hand bend and where it bends to the left, turn right at a public bridleway sign, along a track. This is another curving, partially wooded track which

you follow through several more gates and from which there are again superb views over the Vale to be enjoyed. After 1¾ miles (2.8km), you go through a metal gate on to a lane **Ⓒ**, turn left and follow the lane as far as Moel Arthur car park **Ⓓ**.

Near the far end of the car park use the gap in the wall on the left, indicated by a fingerpost 'Offa's Dyke Path & Llangwyfan Wood,' and join a steepening path that curls through bracken and heather around the eastern flank of Moel Arthur. As the path levels, a short diversion can be made (left) to explore this fine Iron Age hill fort. To reach the finish line, simply remain on the well-used Offa's Dyke Path, descending steadily via three stiles to gain a lane just a few paces downhill from the car park. ●

SCALE 1:25000 or 2½ INCHES to 1 MILE 4CM to 1KM

| 0 | 200 | 400 | 600 | 800 METRES | 1 | |
|---|-----|-----|-----|-----------|---|---|
| | | | | | | KILOMETRES |
| | | | | | | MILES |
| 0 | 200 | 400 | 600 YARDS | ½ | | |

# Llyn Brenig

| | | GPS waypoints |
|---|---|---|
| **Start** | Llyn Brenig Visitor Centre | 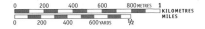 SH 967 546 |
| **Distance** | 10 miles (16.1km) | Ⓐ SH 966 543 |
| **Approximate time** | 4½ hours | Ⓑ SH 978 540 |
| **Parking** | Llyn Brenig Visitor Centre | Ⓒ SH 983 574 |
| **Refreshments** | Café at visitor centre | Ⓓ SH 985 579 |
| **Ordnance Survey maps** | Landranger 116 (Denbigh & Colwyn Bay), Explorer 264 (Vale of Clwyd) | Ⓔ SH 971 581 |
| | | Ⓕ SH 961 571 |

*Llyn Brenig is situated amid the forests and rolling moorlands of Mynydd Hiraethog. This clear and well-waymarked circuit of the reservoir, which mainly uses a mixture of lakeside paths and tracks and forest roads, goes across meadows, over heathery moorland and through the conifer woods of Clocaenog Forest. Although a lengthy walk, the terrain is generally flat and easy, with the likelihood of a few muddy stretches, and there is a succession of fine views across the lake.*

Stand facing the lake in front of the visitor centre and turn right, shortly using a handgate just above the jetty. This gate is marked with a Clwydian Way (CW) disc and also a cream 'walker' disc – these will become familiar as the walk progresses. Walk through to the western end of the stone-clad dam Ⓐ and join the rough road across it.

Ⓑ At the far end turn left, shortly going through a gate. Walk on to a gate (CW) and cattle-grid at the edge of the trees, remaining on the rough road through the woods and beyond around a series of inlets. Hairpin sharp left on the main track (there's an isolated old cottage off to the right) and continue above the reservoir. About 150 yds (137m) before reaching a gate, notice the low, circular stone structure on your left. This is a ring cairn dating from about 1680BC used, it is thought, for funerary rituals. Nearby is a distinct mound – this is Boncyn Arian burial

barrow dating from much the same time.

Ⓒ Use the stile beside the gate and go ahead beside the car park to join a gently rising tarred lane. You're now at the edge of the Gors-Maen-Llŵyd Nature Reserve – there's a bird hide along a path off to your left.

Ⓓ At the top of an incline, look on the left behind a rough lay-by for a waymarked post (CW), here picking up a well-walked path across the moorland. This soon curves around the edge of a wooded area and comes to roughly parallel the main road. There are regular CW posts, although the path is hard to lose.

You'll reach a small, isolated stand of tall ash and short oak trees. Pass immediately left of these and follow the path to a CW post 100 yds (91m) beyond. From here, look ahead to espy a line of

| 0 | 200 | 400 | 600 | 800 METRES | 1 | |
|---|---|---|---|---|---|---|
| | | | | | | KILOMETRES |
| | | | | | | MILES |
| 0 | 200 | 400 | 600 YARDS | | ½ | |

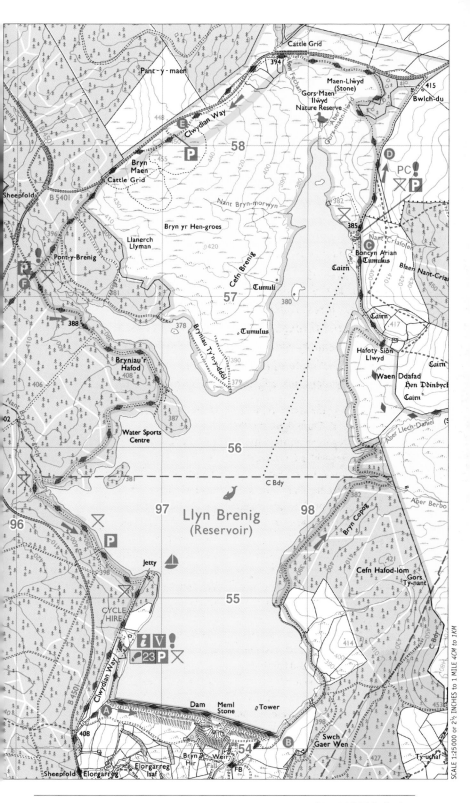

Pant-y-maen

Cattle Grid

394

Clwydian Way

Maen-Llŵyd
(Stone)

Gors-Maen-Llŵyd
Nature Reserve

415

Bwlch-du

58

P

Bryn
Maen
Cattle Grid

Sheepfold

B 5401

448

455

440

420

400

Nant Bryn-morwyn

382

D

PC

P

385

57

Bryn yr Hen-groes

Llanerch
Llyman

0 420

Cefn Brenig

Tumuli

Nant Criafolen

Boncyn Arian
Tumulus

Blaen Nant-Criaf

Cairn

Pont-y-Brenig

P

F

388

381

378

380

Tumulus

Cairn

417

Hafoty Siôn
Llwyd

Cairn

Bryniau Ty'n-y-ddol

390

379

Cairn

Waen Ddafad
Hen Ddinbych

Cairn

Bryniau'r
Hafod
408

387

410

406

Nant Bryn-gors-bach

02

Water Sports
Centre

Aber Llech-Daniel

56

381

C Bdy

Aber Berbo

97

Llyn Brenig
(Reservoir)

98

382

Bryn Copog

96

P

410

400

55

Cefn Hafod-lom
Gors
Ty-nant

421

Jetty

398

CYCLE
HIRE

414

B 5501

Clwydian Way

i V !

23 P

400

C Bdy

453

A

Dam

Meml
Stone

Tower

408

Bryn
Hir

Werr
Fall

FB

54

B

Swch
Gaer Wen

398

Ty-uchaf

427

Sheepfold Elorgarreg

Elorgarreg
Isaf

SCALE 1:25000 or 2½ INCHES to 1 MILE 4CM to 1KM

blue posts; you should take the very narrow path up past these, leaving the main path to curve away left. There are occasional low wooden steps on this path; eventually you'll reach a larger wooden post with a cream 'walker' disc on. Turn right here and walk the heathery path to reach another such post virtually at the roadside fence.

**E** Turn left along the wider, stony path that develops into a track, swinging away from the road and then coming close-by again. There are CW and 'walker' discs confirming the way. Way off to your right, and well beyond the serried ranks of trees forming Alwen Forest, you should be able to pick out the gaunt, hilltop ruins of Gwylfa Hiraethog. This, 'The Wooden Palace', was built in 1908 as a shooting lodge

by the wealthy Lord Davenport, and was claimed (somewhat spuriously) to be the highest inhabited building in Britain at that time. Near a cattle-grid, the path angles away from the road one final time, shortly reaching a handgate giving access to this part of Clocaenog Forest. Keep ahead along the forestry road, which shortly becomes tarred. Cross the solid stone bridge over the Afon Brenig and rise to a crossroads.

**F** Turn left here with the tarred road, remaining on this as it weaves alongside inlets and along promontories to a junction and a 'No Entry' road sign. Keep ahead through the redundant barrier here, passing the sailing club to return to the visitor centre car park.  ●

*A corner of Llyn Brenig*

# Llangollen, Castell Dinas Bran and Valle Crucis Abbey

| | | | GPS waypoints |
|---|---|---|---|
| **Start** | Llangollen | | 🔖 SJ 215 421 |
| **Distance** | 8½ miles (13.7km) | | Ⓐ SJ 223 430 |
| **Approximate time** | 5 hours | | Ⓑ SJ 227 432 |
| **Parking** | Llangollen | | Ⓒ SJ 215 458 |
| **Refreshments** | Pubs and cafés at Llangollen | | Ⓓ SJ 208 458 |
| **Ordnance Survey maps** | Landrangers 117 (Chester & Wrexham) and 125 (Bala & Lake Vyrnwy), Explorers 255 (Llangollen & Berwyn) and 256 (Wrexham) | | Ⓔ SJ 205 441 |
| | | | Ⓕ SJ 203 439 |
| | | | Ⓖ SJ 194 436 |

*This is one of the great classic walks of North Wales with stunning views of the Vale of Llangollen and the Berwyn Mountains, plus plenty of scenic variety and considerable historic interest. Initially there is a steep climb to the scanty remains of Castell Dinas Bran, a superb viewpoint above Llangollen, followed by a rather easier descent and a lovely walk below the limestone cliffs of Eglwyseg, curving round to the substantial ruins of Valle Crucis Abbey. The route continues over Velvet Hill to the Horseshoe Falls on the River Dee, and the final stretch is a relaxing stroll through the valley along the towpath of the Shropshire Union Canal.*

Surrounded by hills and famed as the venue for the annual International Musical Eisteddfod, Llangollen is an excellent touring and walking centre. It lies on the banks of the River Dee, spanned by a 14th-century bridge which is one of the 'Seven Wonders of Wales'. Nearby is the old church of St Collen from which the town gets its name. The black and white house of Plas Newydd and its gardens, home of the Ladies of Llangollen, is just to the south. The two ladies, Eleanor Butler and Sarah Ponsonby, eloped here in the early 19th century and over the years

entertained many of the leading political and literary figures of the time, including the Duke of Wellington, William Wordsworth and Sir Walter Scott. Among Llangollen's other attractions are a ride on the steam-hauled Llangollen Railway, boat trips, (some horse-drawn) along the Shropshire Union Canal, canoeing and white-water rafting trips and a Motor Museum.

🔖 The walk begins at the south end of Llangollen Bridge. Cross the bridge, turn right and then turn left up Wharf Hill, crossing the canal bridge, to reach

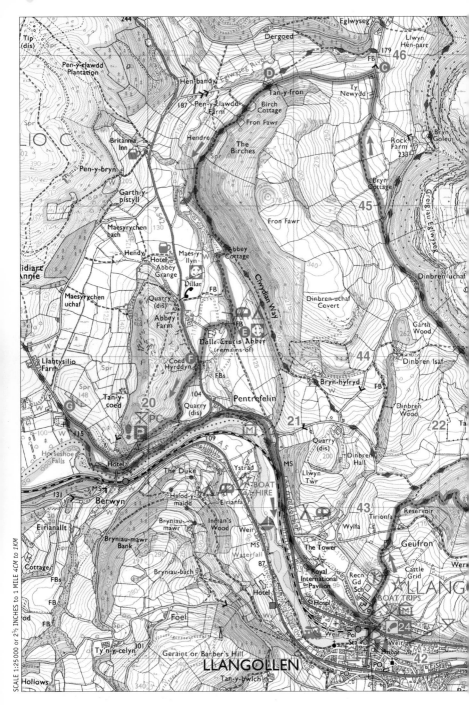

a T-junction. Go up the steps ahead, at a public footpath sign to Offa's Dyke Path Link and walk along an enclosed path.

The first part of the walk to the castle is all uphill. Cross a track by school buildings, continue along a steadily ascending path and, after passing through a kissing-gate, the going becomes steeper as you keep along the

right edge of a field to another kissing-gate.

Go through, continue along a track, keep ahead at a crossroads, go through a kissing-gate and bear right. The route continues across a flat, grassy plateau before the final, steep, zigzag pull up to the summit of the conical hill crowned by the scanty remains of Castell Dinas Bran Ⓐ. There was originally a prehistoric hillfort on the site but the present ruins are those of a 13th-century castle established by the princes of Powys. The magnificent views more than compensate for the effort; they include the Berwyn Mountains, Eglwyseg Cliffs and Llangollen, and extend along the Dee Valley to the Pontcysyllte Aqueduct and across the English border into Shropshire.

Walk east from the castle, roughly in-line with the River Dee, to find a stony path dropping through the ramparts to a kissing-gate (waymarked Clwydian Way). Once through this, the grassy path descends the steep hillside to reach a kissing-gate into a lane, along which turn left.

Ⓑ Cross the cattle-grid and turn left, a National Trail logo (acorn) confirming the route of Offa's Dyke Path. Remain on this undulating lane, which traces the foot of the towering limestone scarp face of Creig iau Eglwyseg for the next 1¼ miles (2km). Pass by two farms and then a road (signed Llangollen) coming in from the left. About 100 yds (91m) past this junction, fork left along a rough farm road, climb a stile beside a gate and walk down to a point immediately before a steel barn. Look carefully for the waymarked, rickety stile just to the right of this (off the grassy track), climb it and trace the left-edge of the long, sloping field to a corner stile. Cross the flat bridge here and continue along the left edge of a field and just before reaching the corner, bear right and head across to a footpath post. Go through a gap in a line of trees, keep by a wire fence on the left and go through a metal gate to rejoin the lane.

Bear left, take the first turning on the left Ⓒ and after ½ mile (0.8km) – where the lane descends to a farm and bends right – bear left on to a track, at a public footpath sign to Valle Crucis Abbey Ⓓ. This firm access track passes remote cottages as it undulates along the side of the Eglwyseg Valley, eventually passing above thick conifers and below superb oakwoods. At a fingerpost for Valle Crucis keep right, descending to a ladder-stile. Climb it, keep ahead and in front of a cottage turn left over another ladder-stile. Walk along the right edge of a field, climb a stile and a few yards ahead, turn right Ⓔ and descend a flight of steps to a footbridge over the River Eglwyseg. Cross it, continue through a caravan site, picking up a track, and go through a gate on to a tarmac drive. To the left are the beautiful ruins of Valle Crucis Abbey, the finest in North Wales, a Cistercian monastery founded in 1201 by the princes of Powys. Much of the church survives, including the fine west

*Valle Crucis Abbey*

front and east end. Among the other buildings grouped around the cloister, the elegantly vaulted chapter house is particularly outstanding. Walk along the drive, passing in front of the abbey, and where it bears left, keep ahead through a kissing-gate, at a public footpath sign to Velvet Hill, and head diagonally across a field. Go through a kissing-gate in the far corner, turn left along a road, carefully cross it and in 100 yds (91m) take the steep path right **F** signed for Llantysilio church. Climb through thick bracken and over a stile into the National Trust's Velvet Hill property, to reach a fingerpost. Keep left here, initially alongside a fence and simply favour the level path, which contours around the hillside before gradually descending as an occasionally narrow and crumbling path through bracken to a stile into birch woods. Take this and drop down to a lane at a junction.

Turn right along the wider lane *(N.B.*

*– not the narrow option sharp right),* shortly signed for Llantysilio and Rhewl and pass above the parking and picnic area at Llantysilio Green. The lane rises easily, revealing fine views across the Horseshoe Falls and the wooded valley of the Dee.

**G** At a fingerpost for 'Canal' turn left down the driveway to Llantysilio church, joining a well-walked path immediately left of the lychgate. The 15th century church is, sadly, usually locked. The path falls to a riverside section, passing beside the Horseshoe Falls. This curving weir, engineered by Thomas Telford, was constructed in 1806 to divert water into the new Llangollen branch of the Shropshire Union Canal system. A metal gate by the gauge house gives access to a waterside path, which is followed for a tranquil 2-mile (3.2km) stretch back to Llangollen. On reaching Llangollen Wharf, fork right at a bollard down a tarred path, descending to the main road above the railway station. Turn left and then cross the Dee Bridge to return to the town centre. ●

# Cilcain and Moel Famau

| | | GPS waypoints | |
|---|---|---|---|
| **Start** | Loggerheads Country Park | 🖋 | SJ 198 626 |
| **Distance** | 8 miles (12.9km) | Ⓐ | SJ 189 652 |
| **Approximate time** | 5 hours | Ⓑ | SJ 177 648 |
| **Parking** | Loggerheads Country Park | Ⓒ | SJ 176 651 |
| **Refreshments** | Café at Country Park, pub at | Ⓓ | SJ 171 647 |
| | Loggerheads, pub at Cilcain | Ⓔ | SJ 161 626 |
| **Ordnance Survey maps** | Landranger 116 (Denbigh & | Ⓕ | SJ 174 629 |
| | Colwyn Bay), Explorer 265 | Ⓖ | SJ 189 627 |
| | (Clwydian Range) | | |

*This lengthy and highly enjoyable walk includes an ascent of Moel Famau, at 1,818 feet (554m) the highest point on the Clwydian Hills and a magnificent viewpoint. The first part of the route is along a most attractive path, the Leete Path, which runs along the side of the wooded Alyn Valley. It continues into Cilcain and descends from the village, after which comes the long, steady and, towards the end, steep climb across open moorland to the summit of Moel Famau. The descent, through the conifers of Clwyd Forest, is reasonably easy and straightforward.*

It is thought that the name 'Logger-heads' may have originated from a lengthy feud in the 18th century between two local landowners over estate boundaries and mineral rights.

🖋 Start by walking in front of the information centre and café, cross a bridge over the River Alyn and turn left along a riverside path signed for The Leete Path and Devil's Gorge. This wide, well-maintained path imperceptibly rises above the river. Keep right at a 'No.4' post and remain on the main path, eventually leaving Loggerheads Country Park via a wall gap and 'No.7' post *(N.B. – do not climb the steps here)*. The Leete Path gets its name from a leat (channel) built in 1823 to carry water to waterwheels at local mills – the Afon Alyn here largely dries up in summer as it flows across limestone, its flow continuing only deep underground; the

leat was built to circumvent this problem.

In 500 yds (457m) use the kissing-gate above kennels (ignore the 'Private' sign, it is a public footpath) and keep ahead on a rough lane. Where this meets a tarred lane, cross diagonally onto a woodland path (signed 'Leete Path and Cilcain') and continue beside the obvious old leat. In about $^3/_4$ mile (1.2km) you'll reach a point where the leat passes beneath the path (there's a stone culvert arch visible on your right). At this point fork left, remaining on the level path beside the leat. In a short distance a protected footbridge passes over the spectacular defile of Devil's Gorge, an old calcite mine. Remain on the narrowing path *(some sheer drops here)*, keeping ahead at any path junctions to reach a minor road.

Ⓐ Turn downhill and wind with the

lane to cross a narrow bridge. Continue beyond for a further 250 yds (228m), rising to a sharp-right bend. Here fork left along a footpath *(N.B. – not the bridleway)* waymarked as the Clwydian Way, joining a narrow path through woods above the Nant Gain. This soon enters pastures; simply keep to the left edge and take a series of stiles. You'll eventually reach an area of recently planted rowan trees and a waymarked gap in the fence on your left. Slip through this and turn right with the path, gradually descending to a junction with a bridleway. Turn right and walk this wider way up to a lane.

**B** Turn right to follow the lane into Cilcain village centre. Bear left to pass in front of the White Horse Inn and then pass right of the church. This mainly 14th - and 15th-century building is noted for its complex and richly decorated nave roof. Too elaborate for a small village church, it is believed to have been brought here from a larger church, perhaps a dissolved abbey, during the Reformation, but its exact origins are a mystery. After passing the church, turn left again **C** along a lane that heads downhill.

**D** At the very sharp left bend, look right for the access drive for Tyddyn y Foel Farm (there's also an open gate and stile here). Walk up this a few paces and then take the waymarked (Clwydian Way) stone stile on the right. Keep to the left edge of two long fields to reach a stile into a rough lane. Here join the gently rising bridleway virtually opposite, soon keeping to the right of the reservoir enclosure, then pass through a gate into open access country. Keep ahead with the main track through trees and bracken, later climbing more steeply across open, heathery moorland to a crossroads at the edge of a conifer plantation. Continue along the right edge of the conifers up to the Jubilee Tower

on the summit of Moel Famau **E** to enjoy the magnificent and extensive view over the Vale of Clwyd. The rather squat tower, built in 1810 to commemorate George III's Golden Jubilee, was originally much higher but was partially destroyed by a severe storm in 1862.

From the tower walk past the nearby triangulation pillar to a stile with the destination 'Loggerheads' rowted in it. Use this and join the track ahead which descends, often steeply, through heath and woods, following signs for Loggerheads across a forestry road and

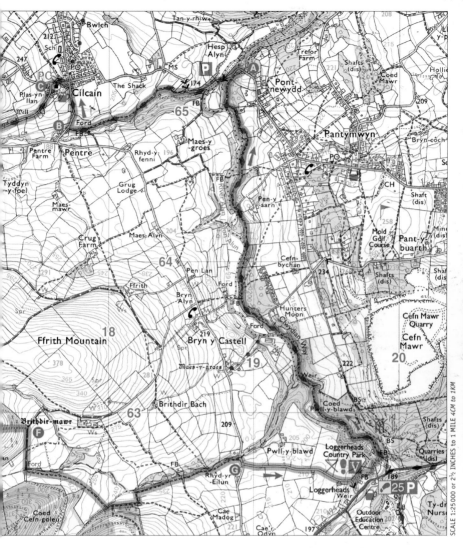

SCALE 1:25000 or 2½ INCHES to 1 MILE 4CM to 1KM

down to a stile at a heavily waymarked
T-junction.

**F** Turn right and walk down to the
bottom gate and a shallow ford. Once
through this turn left along the left edge
of a field to reach a tall waymarked
post. Bear half right on a walked path,
eventually reaching a sleeper bridge
and a mossy fingerpost. Walk up to the
nearby stile but do not cross it; instead
turn left to another stile and climb this,
then walk the foot of the cleared
woodland to a further stile. Climb this
and head right to a fingerposted stile.

Turn down the enclosed track and turn
right at the bend (all route furniture is
signed for Loggerheads) along the edge
of a field. Pass through a hedge gap and
keep ahead, hedge now on your right,
remaining on this old field road through
a stile and two metal gates to gain a
tarred lane. **G** Turn right; at the nearby
junction turn left and walk the ½ mile
(800m) to a path on the left cutting
through to Loggerheads car park. ●

# Bwlch Maen Gwynedd

| | | | |
|---|---|---|---|
| **Start** | Llandrillo | **GPS waypoints** | |
| **Distance** | 7¾ miles (12.5km) | ⬛ SJ 035 371 | |
| **Approximate time** | 5 hours | Ⓐ SJ 037 369 | |
| **Parking** | Llandrillo | Ⓑ SJ 043 352 | |
| **Refreshments** | Pub, restaurant and village stores in Llandrillo | Ⓒ SJ 076 341 | |
| | | Ⓓ SJ 051 375 | |
| **Ordnance Survey maps** | Landranger 125 (Bala & Lake Vyrnwy), Explorer 255 (Llangollen & Berwyn) | | |

*The walk leads through austere and lonely terrain into the heart of the Berwyn Mountains to Bwlch Maen Gwynedd, a gap in the long ridge between Cadair Bronwen and Cadair Berwyn, two of the highest peaks in the range. Bwlch Maen Gwynedd itself is at 2,330 feet (710m) and from it the views, along the ridge and down into the valleys on both sides, are awe-inspiring. On the outward route some sections of the path are indistinct and you have to avoid a boggy area. The return is along a much clearer and easier track, but* this walk does involve rough walking across open moorland and hillside and should not be attempted in bad weather, especially misty conditions, unless you are an experienced hill walker able to navigate by using a compass.

Llandrillo is attractively situated on the Afon Ceidiog, a tributary of the River Dee, and from the bridge there is a fine view of the tower and spire of the church rising above the village.

🖊 From the car park entrance turn left along the main road. Cross to the village hall (Y Ganolfan) and take the waymarked path that passes to the right of the building. Cross a stile and walk along an enclosed path, use another stile and keep ahead along the right-hand edge of a field. From the offset hedge corner and oak tree, look left to locate a stile and fingerpost next to a field gate; join a lane here.

Ⓐ Turn right along the lane, go through a gate and start a gradual climb, passing to the left of Llechwedd farmhouse and up a green track to an old metal field gate at the foot of woodland. Join the track beyond this, skirting the woods and passing through another metal gate. At a junction bear left, taking a wooden gate and rising along the track to a fork. Keep left here; the track steepens before emerging from the woods at a sharp left bend. On the right here are two gates; take the lower one and follow the old sunken lane as it rises gradually towards the high moors.

Ⓑ Go through a gate and, a few paces farther on, climb the stone stile beside a gate at the border of Open Access country – there's also a bridleway fingerpost for Craig Berwyn here and a National Nature Reserve board for Y Berwyn Reserve. Walk ahead on the

*Moel Ty-uchaf stone circle*

declining track, with a wall on your right. The next ½ mile (800m) or so may be waterlogged in places. The track descends towards a stream (Clochnant); at this stage it is important to bear left away from the stream in order to avoid a marshy area ahead, Gwern Wynodl. The path tends to peter out here but aim for the higher, drier, heathery moorland to the left, later bearing right back towards the stream and making for the distinct landmark of a small, rectangular conifer wood clearly seen ahead. As you head towards it, a definite path appears again and you continue to a metal gate. Go through, keep ahead, passing along the right edge of the conifer wood, ford a stream and continue along a clear and obvious path that climbs gently above Clochnant. Ahead is an impressive view

looking towards the head of the valley and the Berwyn ridge. At a fork take the right-hand lower path, ford a tributary stream and continue uphill. The path briefly becomes soggy and indistinct again and this is quite a tiring part of the walk, but you eventually reach a metal gate at the top of the pass, Bwlch Maen Gwynedd, 2,330ft (710m) high **C**. Go through and keep ahead a few yards to enjoy a magnificent view: to the right along the Berwyn ridge to Cadair Berwyn, to the left along the ridge to Cadair Bronwen, behind to the Dee Valley, and ahead along the steep-sided, sweeping, curving valley of Cwm Maen Gwynedd. Turn back through the gate, retrace your steps for about 100 yards (91m) to a fork – probably not noticed on the way up – and take the right-hand path which can be seen heading up over the slopes in front. The path descends

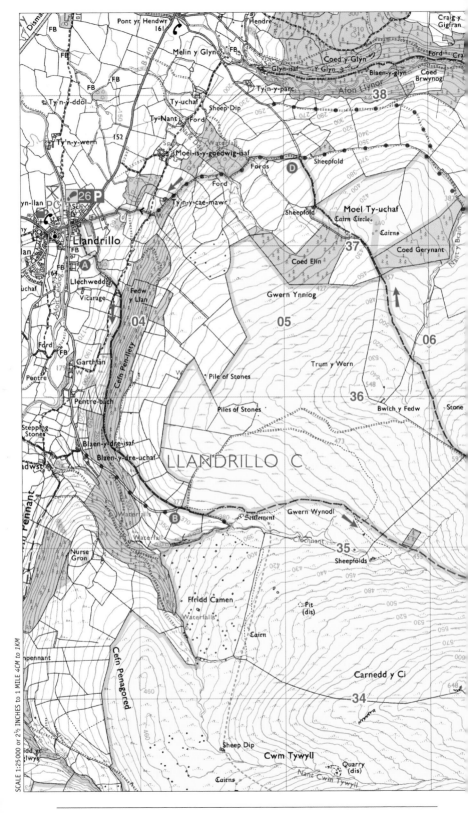

SCALE 1:25 000 or 2½ INCHES to 1 MILE 4CM to 1KM

initially, then continues gently up, later bearing right and curving left above the head of Blaen Trawsnant. From here there is a superb view to the left of Cadair Berwyn. Continue gently up over Moel Pearce along what has become an undulating track, joining and keeping by a wire fence on the right, and on arriving at two metal gates, go through the right-hand one. The track gradually bends right, away from the fence. Go through a gate, beyond which the track braids; your target is the plantation of fir trees ahead. Two gates take you alongside the left edge of these. After the second one, look to your right to spot a stone circle on a low hilltop. It's

well worth climbing up to this to enjoy the impressive views and the excellent condition of this evocative Bronze Age monument on Moel Ty-uchaf. From here, head back down a sheep track to regain the fieldside track and walk to a corner and two gates. Use the right-hand one, walking beside a wall on your left through to several gates at a crossing of paths and tracks.

Ⓓ The track ahead becomes tarred beyond a gate. You do not want this one, however. Instead, take the wide gate on your left and join a field road bordered by widely spaced fences and walls. Simply remain on this, going through several bridgegates and across a couple of shallow fords above woodland. At a junction fork right, downhill along a stonier track. Pass through another gate to reach a junction near a farmhouse. Keep ahead here, passing above the house on a wide path beside a wall and within the edge of oak woods. A final gate leads to the top of a steep tarred lane; following this brings you back to Llandrillo's war memorial near the village hall. ●

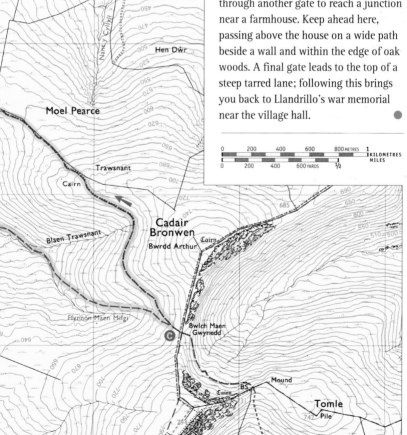

# Carnedd Dafydd

| | | GPS waypoints |
|---|---|---|
| Start | Ogwen, at western end of Llyn Ogwen. Shorter version starts at the eastern end of the lake | SH 649 603 |
| | | (A) SH 649 605 |
| Distance | 7 miles (11.3km). Shorter version 5½ miles (8.9km) | (B) SH 667 608 |
| | | (C) SH 666 617 |
| Approximate time | 6 hours (5 hours for shorter version) | (D) SH 654 620 |
| | | (E) SH 663 630 |
| Parking | Ogwen. For shorter walk there are plenty of lay-bys alongside and beyond eastern end of the lake | (F) SH 666 630 |
| Refreshments | Kiosk at Ogwen | |
| Ordnance Survey maps | Landranger 115 (Snowdon), Explorer OL17 (Snowdon – Conwy Valley) | |

*At 3,425 feet (1,044m) Carnedd Dafydd is one of the highest peaks in the Carneddau range and a magnificent viewpoint. After an initial walk, rocky and wet in places, along the north shore of Llyn Ogwen, there follows a fairly steep climb beside the Afon Lloer. The route then curves left and continues more steeply uphill, with some rough scrambling, to the 3,211-ft (978m) summit of Pen yr Ole Wen. From there an easy ridge path leads on to Carnedd Dafydd. Continuing along the ridge towards Carnedd Llewelyn for a short distance, the walk then drops through boulders and across grassy slopes offering mouthwatering views of Tryfan and the Glyders. The shorter route omits the somewhat boggy walk along the northern shore of Llyn Ogwen.*

This walk involves some simple scrambling and is thus best suited to those with experience of such. In addition, it includes some of the highest ground in Snowdonia and should not be attempted in bad weather, misty or snowy conditions unless you are adequately equipped and able to use a map and compass. In wet weather the route will be very slippery underfoot in places.

From the car park at the west end of Llyn Ogwen, return to the main road and turn left. Cross over, cross the river bridge and take the waymarked stile on the right.

(A) Bear right along a narrow path, immediately meeting the first of many agile scrambles on the walk, around a rock face above the river. The path threads amidst boulders, rocks and vegetation to a ladder-stile. Beyond this the main path gradually heads left away

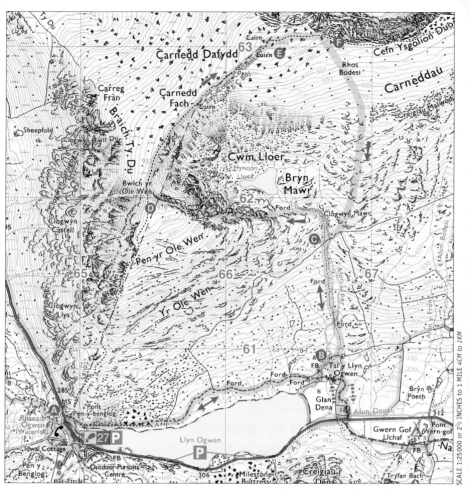

from the shoreline of Llyn Ogwen. It passes through a gap in a wall and then braids through damp and marshy country, initially to the left of the line of wires but mostly to the right of them, en route crossing several small streams. You eventually reach a ladder-stile over a fence. Continue on the level ahead, past waymark posts to climb another ladder-stile just above a stand of firs and a farmhouse. Cross the footbridge and go ahead to the third waymark post, just 20 paces before a ladder-stile over a wall. Here turn left (do not climb the stile), uphill on a slabbed path.

*This is where the shorter walk joins*

the main route. If you start from one of the lay-bys at the eastern end of Llyn Ogwen, walk east along the left side of the road to find a rough driveway on the left, marked 'Private Road'. Turn along this, cross the river bridge and go past the bungalow to a stile and cattle-grid. Wind with the track beyond to the entrance gate to the farm. Here turn right, putting the wall on your left. Shortly, climb a ladder-stile on your left and walk ahead to the first waymark post. Turn right uphill on the slabbed path.

**B** The path rises past a series of waymark posts, most of which are posts with cream bands painted on; some are leaning while others lie buried in bracken. You'll rise constantly, soon crossing and re-crossing the braided

*Tryfan from Pen yr Ole Wen*

rivulets of the Afon Lloer several times. The appropriate route is, so far as you can, to keep near to the left bank. This will bring you to a ladder-stile about 30 yds (27m) west of the river as it passes beneath a wall.

**C** Climb the stile and continue up beside the river; in about 200 yds (183m) this path curves left away from the water on a course improved by National Trust and National Park staff and volunteers by strengthening it with boulders. The path becomes increasingly indistinct as you approach crags – well off to your right you'll see the lake of Ffynnon Lloer nestling below the immense screes of Cwm Lloer. There's no single recognisable path up through these crags, and whichever route you choose you'll find it necessary to indulge in some easy scrambling. Keeping slightly left is the best option and occasional small cairns mark a ghost of a path up the crags. The scrambling gives way to a wide path rising steeply above the edge of the screes, eventually gaining the small summit plateau of Pen yr Ole Wen with its vandalised cairn. Your reward is immense views to all points of the compass – across Anglesey, over the

Glyders to Snowdon and along the Llŷn Peninsula, south across the entire depth of Snowdonia and east along the bleak ridge of the Carneddau.

**D** Keep the sheer drop on your right and walk ahead from the cairn to join a wide, well-worn path curving right to join the ridge path. It descends for a short while before rising over a huge cairn/pile of boulders and continuing to climb to the modest cairn at the summit of Carnedd Dafydd, about one mile (1.6km) from **D**.

**E** Bear right from here along the continuing ridge path that heads towards the distant summit of Carnedd Llewelyn. You'll pass a second cairn in 150 yds (137m) and come close to a precipice on your left. **F** At this juncture, start to arc right, leaving the main path and descend through a boulder-field (there's no walked path), beyond this coming to easy grass and bilberry slopes. Down in the valley is the main A5 road and the eastern end of Llyn Ogwen. You should aim to walk towards the second clump of fir trees left of the lake's end. This direction soon brings you to a point where Ffynnon Lloer again comes into view below Carnedd Dafydd and a distinct marshy depression lies at your feet. Keep slightly left here, still descending across pathless terrain and by now heading directly towards the distinct pinnacle of Tryfan.

Depending on how far right you drift, you'll either reach the Afon Lloer (in which case follow it downstream) or follow a low craggy ridge – Clogwyn Mawr – and drop to a cross-wall (in which case turn right alongside it). Either way you'll come to the point where the river passes beneath the wall. Cross the river here and walk on a few paces to climb the ladder-stile you used earlier in the walk at **C**. From here, retrace the outward route back down to your starting point. ●

# Snowdon via the Watkin Path

| | | GPS waypoints |
|---|---|---|
| **Start** | Pont Bethania car park, on A498 between Llyn Dinas and Llyn Gwynant | 🖉 SH 627 506 |
| | | Ⓐ SH 621 520 |
| | | Ⓑ SH 609 542 |
| **Distance** | 9 miles (14.5km) | Ⓒ SH 610 544 |
| **Approximate time** | 7 hours | Ⓓ SH 618 518 |
| **Parking** | Pont Bethania | |
| **Refreshments** | Café at Snowdon summit station (restricted opening) | |
| **Ordnance Survey maps** | Landranger 115 (Snowdon), Explorer OL17 (Snowdon – Conwy Valley) | |

*Of the various alternative routes to the summit of Snowdon, the Watkin Path is one of the longest, but also arguably the most attractive. It is also relatively easy, but nevertheless an ascent of Snowdon must never be underestimated. A long, steady climb along a well-constructed path, passing a series of waterfalls and the remains of abandoned quarries, leads to a final scramble on to the summit ridge. From here it is a short walk to the 3,560 feet (1,085m) summit, the highest point in Britain south of the Scottish Highlands. It is a tremendously exhilarating and satisfying feeling to conquer Snowdon and enjoy what, on a clear day, are the necessarily extensive and magnificent views. The descent, also long and steady rather than steep, is a superb ridge walk, later curving through Cwm Llan to rejoin the Watkin Path.* It must be emphasised that on no account should this walk be attempted in bad weather or during the winter months, unless you are experienced in such conditions, able to navigate by using a compass and possess the right clothing, footwear and equipment.

*It is the nature of Snowdon that there are precipitous drops on all approaches to the summit. On the Watkin Path these are met approaching the summit ridge and also on the return leg along Bwlch Main and Clogwyn Du.* If you do not have a good head for heights, then we recommend that you do not do this walk.

🖉 Turn left from the car park, cross the road and take the tarred lane on the right in 50 yds (46m), signed as the entrance to the National Trust's Hafod-y-llan Estate. In a few paces take the steps, signed as the Watkin Path, up to a

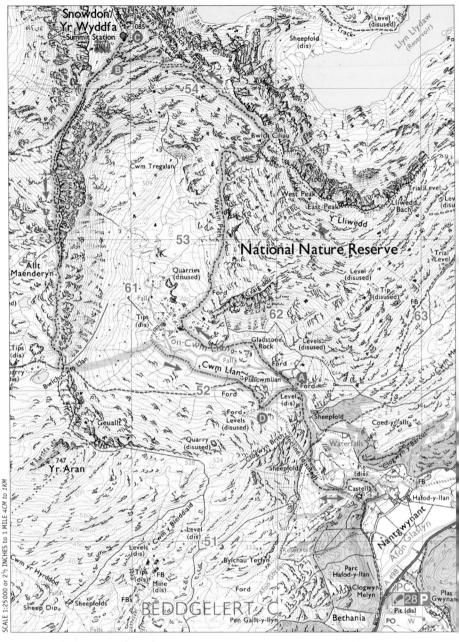

| | | | | | |
|---|---|---|---|---|---|
| 0 | 200 | 400 | 600 | 800 METRES | 1 |

KILOMETRES
MILES

| | | | | |
|---|---|---|---|---|
| 0 | 200 | 400 | 600 YARDS | ½ |

handgate. Beyond, a gravelled path meanders gradually uphill through splendid oak woods, occasional steps, two footbridges and another handgate leading you to a metal gate onto a rough stony track. Bear left, go through another metal gate and follow the track steadily uphill and over a flatbridge **Ⓐ**, shortly passing the Gladstone Rock. At the age of 84, William Gladstone made a speech here at the opening of the Watkin Path in 1892. Soon the ascent becomes steeper, the views become more magnificent and a series of cairns marks the way. Finally you climb a steep, zigzag path – not always clearly defined – which involves some modest scrambling, to emerge on to a ridge by a large rock . Turn right for the short distance to the summit station and café, and beyond that the summit cairn itself .

The views are, of course, magnificent and extend over the rest of Snowdonia and much of North Wales. In exceptionally clear conditions they can embrace the Wicklow Mountains in Ireland, the Isle of Man and some of the higher Lake District peaks. The Snowdon Mountain Railway, a great triumph of Victorian engineering, is the only rack-and-pinion railway in Britain and was opened to passenger traffic in 1896. The journey from Llanberis to the summit of Snowdon is about five miles (8km) long, with an average gradient of 1 in 7.

From the summit retrace your steps to where you joined the ridge and continue along the ridge path. In clear weather the Watkin Path can be seen over to the left and even the starting

*Heading up the Watkin Path on the ascent of Yr Wyddfa – Snowdon itself*

point in the Nantgwynant Valley is visible far below. At a fork take the left-hand uphill path which later descends – a winding, rocky and quite difficult descent in places – to a ladder-stile. Climb it, continue downhill into a col and follow the path to the left to go through a wall-gap.

Beyond this gap, the way becomes less steep, developing into a grassy path heading towards the old mine workings near the head of Cwm Llan. Just before reaching these you'll meet the course of a dismantled tramway that once carried the copper ore mined in this great bowl below Snowdon down into Nantgwynant. Turn right and walk along this old tramway for about $^1/_2$ mile (800m). Just after passing through a very short cutting, the track bends left. Here turn left off the level path (the tramway becomes noticeably grassier beyond this point) onto a path which drops down beside a stream to join the outward route at beside the Afon Cwm Llan, not far below a bridge and directly across the river from old mine buildings. Turn right and retrace your outward route back to the start.  ●

# Further Information

 ## The National Trust

Anyone who likes visiting places of natural beauty and/or historic interest has cause to be grateful to the National Trust. Without it, many such places would probably have vanished by now.

The purpose of the National Trust is to preserve areas of natural beauty and sites of historic interest by acquisition, holding them in trust for the nation and making them available for public access and enjoyment. Some of its properties have been acquired through purchase, but many of the Trust's properties have been donated. Nowadays it is not only one of the biggest landowners in the country, but also one of the most active conservation charities, protecting 581,113 acres (253,176 ha) of land, including 555 miles (892km) of coastline, and over 300 historic properties in England, Wales and Northern Ireland. (There is a separate National Trust for Scotland, which was set up in 1931.)

For details of membership, contact the National Trust at the address on page 95.

 ## The Ramblers' Association

No organisation works more actively to protect and extend the rights and interests of walkers in the countryside than the Ramblers' Association. Its aims are clear: to foster a greater knowledge, love and care of the countryside; to assist in the protection and enhancement of public rights of way and areas of natural beauty; to work for greater public access to the countryside; and to encourage more people to take up rambling as a healthy, recreational leisure activity.

It was founded in 1935 when, following the setting up of a National Council of Ramblers' Federations in 1931, a number of federations earlier formed in London, Manchester, the Midlands and elsewhere came together to create a more effective pressure group, to deal with such problems as the disappearance and obstruction of footpaths, the prevention of access to open mountain and moorland and increasing hostility from landowners. This was the era of the mass trespasses, when there were sometimes violent confrontations between ramblers and gamekeepers, especially on the moorlands of the Peak District.

Since then the Ramblers' Association has played an influential role in preserving and developing the national footpath network, supporting the creation of national parks and encouraging the designation and waymarking of long-distance routes.

Our freedom to walk in the countryside is precarious and requires constant vigilance. As well as the perennial problems of footpaths being illegally obstructed, disappearing through lack of use or extinguished by housing or road construction, new dangers can spring up at any time.

It is to meet such problems and dangers that the Ramblers' Association exists and represents the interests of all walkers. The address to write to for information on the Ramblers' Association and how to become a member is given on page 95.

 ## Walkers and the Law

The *Countryside and Rights of Way Act 2000 (CRoW)* extends the rights of access previously enjoyed by walkers in England and Wales. Implementation of these rights began on 19 September 2004. The Act amends existing legislation and for the first time provides access on foot to certain types of land – defined as mountain, moor, heath, down and registered common land.

*Where You Can Go*
**Rights of Way**
Prior to the introduction of CRoW walkers could only legally access the countryside along public rights of way. These are either 'footpaths' (for walkers only) or 'bridleways'

(for walkers, riders on horseback and pedal cyclists). A third category called 'Byways open to all traffic' (BOATs), is used by motorised vehicles as well as those using non-mechanised transport. Mainly they are green lanes, farm and estate roads, although occasionally they will be found crossing mountainous area.

Rights of way are marked on Ordnance Survey maps. Look for the green broken lines on the Explorer maps, or the red dashed lines on Landranger maps.

The term 'right of way' means exactly what it says. It gives a right of passage over what, for the most part, is private land. Under pre-CRoW legislation walkers were required to keep to the line of the right of way and not stray onto land on either side. If you did inadvertently wander off the right of way, either because of faulty map reading or because the route was not clearly indicated on the ground, you were technically trespassing.

Local authorities have a legal obligation to ensure that rights of way are kept clear and free of obstruction, and are signposted where they leave metalled roads. The duty of local authorities to install signposts extends to the placing of signs along a path or way, but only where the authority considers it necessary to have a signpost or waymark to assist persons unfamiliar with the locality.

### The New Access Rights
### Access Land
As well as being able to walk on existing rights of way, under the new legislation you now have access to large areas of open land. You can of course continue to use rights of way footpaths to cross this land, but the main difference is that you can now law-fully leave the path and wander at will, but only in areas designated as access land.

### Where to Walk
Areas now covered by the new access rights – Access Land – are shown on Ordnance Survey Explorer maps bearing 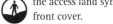 the access land symbol on the front cover.

Access Land' is shown on Ordnance Survey maps by a light yellow tint surrounded by a pale orange border. New orange coloured 'i' symbols on the maps will show the location of permanent access information boards installed by the access authorities.

### Restrictions
The right to walk on access land may lawfully be restricted by landowners. Landowners can, for any reason, restrict access for up to 28 days in any year. They cannot however close the land:

- on bank holidays;
- for more than four Saturdays and Sundays in a year;
- on any Saturday from 1 June to 11 August; or
- on any Sunday from 1 June to the end of September.

They have to provide local authorities with five working days' notice before the date of closure unless the land involved is an area of less than five hectares or the closure is for less than four hours. In these cases landowners only need to provide two hours' notice.

Whatever restrictions are put into place on access land they have no effect on existing rights of way, and you can continue to walk on them.

### Dogs
Dogs can be taken on access land, but must be kept on leads of two metres or less between 1 March and 31 July, and at all times where they are near livestock. In addition landowners may impose a ban on all dogs from fields where lambing takes place for up to six weeks in any year. Dogs may be banned from moorland used for grouse shooting and breeding for up to five years.

In the main, walkers following the routes in this book will continue to follow existing rights of way, but a knowledge and understanding of the law as it affects walkers, plus the ability to distinguish access land marked on the maps, will enable anyone who wishes to depart from paths that cross access land either to take a shortcut, to enjoy a view or to explore.

*Further Information*

## General Obstructions

Obstructions can sometimes cause a problem on a walk and the most common of these is where the path across a field has been ploughed over. It is legal for a farmer to plough up a path provided that it is restored within two weeks. This does not always happen and you are faced with the dilemma of following the line of the path, even if this means treading on crops, or walking round the edge of the field. Although the later course of action seems the most sensible, it does mean that you would be trespassing.

Other obstructions can vary from overhanging vegetation to wire fences across the path, locked gates or even a cattle feeder on the path.

Use common sense. If you can get round the obstruction without causing damage, do so. Otherwise only remove as much of the obstruction as is necessary to secure passage.

If the right of way is blocked and cannot be followed, there is a long-standing view that in such circumstances there is a right to deviate, but this cannot wholly be relied on. Although it is accepted in law that highways (and that includes rights of way) are for the public service, and if the usual track is impassable, it is for the general good that people should be entitled to pass into another line. However, this should not be taken as indicating a right to deviate whenever a way becomes impassable. If in doubt, retreat.

Report obstructions to the local authority and/or the Ramblers' Association.

### Global Positioning System (GPS)

**What is GPS?**

GPS is a worldwide radio navigation system that uses a network of 24 satellites and receivers, usually hand-held, to calculate positions. By measuring the time it takes a signal to reach the receiver, the distance from the satellite can be estimated. Repeat this with several satellites and the receiver can then use triangulation to establish the position of the receiver.

### Glossary of Welsh Words

This list gives some of the more common elements in Welsh place names, which will allow readers to understand otherwise meaningless words and appreciate the relationship between place names and landscape features. Place names often have variant spellings, and the more common of these are given here.

| | | | |
|---|---|---|---|
| aber | estuary, confluence | foel, moel | rounded hill |
| afon | river | glyn | glen |
| bach, fach | small | hen | old |
| bont, pont | bridge | llan, eglwys | church |
| bryn | mound, hill | llyn | lake |
| bwlch | pass | maen | stone |
| caer | fort | mawr, fawr | big |
| capel | chapel | moel, foel | rounded hill |
| carn, carnedd | cairn | morfa | sea marsh |
| castell | castle | mynydd | mountain |
| ceunant | gorge, ravine | nant | brook |
| coed | wood | newydd | new |
| craig | crag | pair | cauldron |
| crib | narrow ridge | pen | head, top |
| cwm | valley | pont, bont | bridge |
| drws | doors, gap (pass) | pwll | pool |
| dyffryn | valley | rhaedr | waterfall |
| eglwys, llan | church | sarn | causeway |
| fach, bach | small | traeth | beach, shore |
| fawr, mawr | big | twll | hole |
| ffordd | road | ynys | island |

## Countryside Access Charter

*Your rights of way are:*

- public footpaths – on foot only. Sometimes waymarked in yellow
- bridleways – on foot, horseback and pedal cycle. Sometimes waymarked in blue
- byways (usually old roads), most 'roads used as public paths' and, of course, public roads – all traffic has the right of way

Use maps, signs and waymarks to check rights of way. Ordnance Survey Explorer and Landranger maps show most public rights of way

*On rights of way you can:*

- take a pram, pushchair or wheelchair if practicable
- take a dog (on a lead or under close control)
- take a short route round an illegal obstruction or remove it sufficiently to get past

*You have a right to go for recreation to:*

- public parks and open spaces – on foot
- most commons near older towns and cities – on foot and sometimes on horseback
- private land where the owner has a formal agreement with the local authority

*In addition you can use the following by local or established custom or consent, but ask for advice if you are unsure:*

- many areas of open country, such as moorland, fell and coastal areas, especially those in the care of the National Trust, and some commons
- some woods and forests, especially those owned by the Forestry Commission
- country parks and picnic sites
- most beaches
- canal towpaths
- some private paths and tracks Consent sometimes extends to horse-riding and cycling

*For your information:*

- county councils and London boroughs maintain and record rights of way, and register commons
- obstructions, dangerous animals, harassment and misleading signs on rights of way are illegal and you should report them to the county council
- paths across fields can be ploughed, but must normally be reinstated within two weeks
- landowners can require you to leave land to which you have no right of access
- motor vehicles are normally permitted only on roads, byways and some 'roads used as public paths'

### How to use GPS with Ordnance Survey mapping

Each of the walks in this book includes GPS co-ordinate data that reflects the walk position points on Ordnance Survey maps.

GPS and OS maps use different models for the earth and co-ordinate systems, so when you are trying to relate your GPS position to features on the map the two will differ slightly. This is especially the case with height, as the model that relates the GPS global co-ordinate system to height above sea level is very poor.

When using GPS with OS mapping, some distortion – up to 16ft (5m) – will always be present. Moreover, individual features on maps may have been surveyed only to an accuracy of 23ft (7m) (for 1:25000 scale maps), while other features, e.g. boulders, are usually only shown schematically.

In practice, this should not cause undue difficulty, as you will be near enough to your objective to be able to spot it.

### How to use the GPS data in this book

There are various ways you can use the GPS data in this book.

1. Follow the route description while checking your position on your receiver when you are approaching a position point.

2. You can also use the positioning information on your receiver to verify where you are on the map.

*Further Information*

*Further Information*

3. Alternatively, you can use some of the proprietary software that is available. At the simple end there is inexpensive software, which lets you input the walk positions (waypoints), download them to the gps unit and then use them to assist your navigation on the walks.

At the upper end of the market Ordnance Survey maps are available in electronic form. Most come with software that enables you to enter your walking route onto the map, download it to your gps unit and use it, alongside the route description, to follow the route.

 ### Safety on the Hills

The hills, mountains and moorlands of Britain, though of modest height compared with those in many other countries, need to be treated with respect. Friendly and inviting in good weather, they can quickly be transformed into wet, misty, windswept and potentially dangerous areas of wilderness in bad weather. Even on an outwardly fine and settled summer day, conditions can rapidly deteriorate. In winter, of course, the weather can be even more erratic and the hours of daylight are much shorter.

Therefore it is advisable to always take both warm and waterproof clothing, sufficient nourishing food, a hot drink, first-aid kit, torch and whistle. Wear suitable footwear such as strong walking boots or shoes that give a good grip over rocky terrain and on slippery slopes. Try to obtain a local weather forecast and bear it in mind before you start. Do not be afraid to abandon your proposed route and return to your starting point in the event of a sudden and unexpected deterioration in the weather. Do not go alone. Allow enough time to finish the walk well before nightfall.

Most of the walks described in this book do not venture into remote wilderness areas and will be safe to do, given due care and respect, at any time of year in all but the most unreasonable weather. Indeed, a crisp, fine winter day often provides perfect conditions for walking, with firm ground underfoot and a clarity that it is not possible

to achieve in the other seasons of the year. A few walks in this book, however, are suitable only for reasonably fit and experienced hill walkers who are able to use a compass, and these routes should definitely not be tackled by anyone else during the winter months or in bad weather, especially high winds and mist. These are indicated in the general description that precedes each of the walks. Weather forecasts for Snowdonia can be found on the website **www.metoffice.gov.uk** using the links to Mountain Weather and Snowdonia.

 ### Useful Organisations

**Council for National Parks**
6-7 Barnard Mews, London
SW11 1QU
Tel. 020 7924 4077
www.cnp.org.uk

**Snowdonia National Park Authority**
National Park Office, Penrhyndeudraeth, Gwynedd LL48 6LF
Tel. 01766 770274
www.eryi-npa.co.uk
*National Park information centres:*
Aberdyfi: 01654 767321
Betws-y-Coed: 01690 710426
Blaenau Ffestiniog: 01766 830360
Dolgellau: 01341 422888
Harlech: 01766 780658
Llanberis: 01286 870765

**Snowdonia Society**
Ty Hyll, Capel Curig, Conwy
LL24 0DS
Tel. 01690 720287
www.snowdonia-society.org.uk

**Campaign for the Protection of Rural Wales**
Tŷ Gwyn, 31 High Street, Welshpool, Powys SY21 7YD
Tel. 01938 552525/556212
www.cprw.org.uk

**Countryside Council for Wales**
Plas Penrhos, Ffordd Penrhos, Bangor, Gwynedd LL5 72LQ
Tel. 01248 370444
www.countryside.wales.gov.uk

Forestry Commission
Silvan House, 231 Corstorphine Road,
Edinburgh EH12 7AT
Tel. 0131 334 0303
www.forestry.gov.uk

Long Distance Walkers' Association
www.ldwa.org.uk

National Trust
*Membership and general enquiries:*
PO Box 39, Warrington WA5 7WD
Tel. 0870 458 4000
*National Trust Office for Wales*
Trinity Square, Llandudno,
Gwynedd LL30 2DE
Tel. 01492 860123
www.nationaltrust.org.uk

Natural England
Northminster House, Peterborough,
PE1 1UA
Tel. 0845 600 3078
www.naturalengland.org.uk

Ordnance Survey
Romsey Road, Maybush,
Southampton SO16 4GU
Tel. 08456 05 05 05 (Lo-call)
www.ordnancesurvey.co.uk

Ramblers' Association (main office)
2nd Floor, Camelford House,
87–90 Albert Embankment,
London SE1 7TW
Tel. 020 7339 8500
www.ramblers.org.uk

Ramblers' Association (Wales)
3 Coopers Yard, Curran Road,
Cardiff, CF10 5NB
Tel. 029 2064 4308

www.visitwales.com

*Tourist information centres (*not open all year):*
*Bala: 01678 521021
Bangor: 02891 270069
Betws-y-Coed: 01690 710426
*Blaenau Ffestiniog: 01766 830360
*Conwy: 01492 592248
*Corris: 01654 761244

Dolgellau: 01341 422888
*Llanberis: 01286 870765
Llandudno: 01492 876413
Llangollen: 01978 860828
*Mold: 01352 759331
Porthmadog: 01766 512981
Rhyl: 01745 355068
Ruthin: 01824 703992
Wrexham: 01978 292015

Youth Hostels Association
Trevelyan House, Dimple Road,
Matlock, Derbyshire
DE4 3YH
Tel. 01692 592600
www.yha.org.uk

 ## Ordnance Survey maps of Snowdonia

North Wales, Snowdon and Offa's Dyke are
covered by Ordnance Survey 1:50 000
(1¼ inches to 1 mile or 2cm to 1km) scale
Landranger map sheets 115, 116, 117, 124, 125
and 126. These all-purpose maps are packed
with information to help you explore the area
and show viewpoints, picnic sites, places of
interest and caravan and camping sites.

To examine the area in more detail, and
especially if you are planning walks, Ordnance
Survey Explorer maps at 1:25 000 (2½
inches to 1 mile or 4cm to 1km) scale are ideal:

OL17 (Snowdon – Conwy Valley)
OL18 (Harlech, Porthmadog & Bala)
OL23 (Cadair Idris & Llyn Tegid)
240 (Oswestry)
255 (Llangollen & Berwyn)
256 (Wrexham)
264 (Vale of Clwyd)
265 (Clwydian Range)
266 (Wirral & Chester)

To get to North Wales use the Ordnance
Survey OS Travel Map-Route Great Britain
at 1:625 000 (1 inch to 10 miles or 4cm to
25km) scale or Ordnance Survey OS Travel
Map-Road 6 (Wales and West Midlands) at
1:250 000 (1 inch to 4 miles or 1cm to
2.5km) scale.

Ordnance Survey maps and guides are
available from most booksellers, stationers
and newsagents.